In Foreign Parts

CANTERBURY SOURCES 2

SHEIKH NÂSIR.
The religious head of the Yeseedees.

Sheikh Nâsir, the religious head of the Yeseedees
(George Percy Badger, *The Nestorians and their rituals*, 1852)

CANTERBURY SOURCES 2

In Foreign Parts

Books and pamphlets
on the world beyond Western Europe
printed before 1900
in Canterbury Cathedral Library

compiled by
Helen Southwood

revised by David Shaw

with an Introduction
by
Glenn Bowman

CANTERBURY
2000

CANTERBURY SOURCES
is published by
the Dean and Chapter, Canterbury Cathedral.

General Editor: David J. Shaw

The CANTERBURY SOURCES device
on the title-page is based on the second seal
of the Cathedral Priory in use from the 1150s to the 1220s
(Cathedral Archives, DCc/Charta Antiqua C 163).

The illustration on the front cover is from J. Nieuhof, *Voyages
and travels, into Brasil, and the East-Indies*, 1703, IFP325.

ISBN 0950 13923 8

Typeset by David J. Shaw
Printed by Thanet Press

CANTERBURY SOURCES
Canterbury Cathedral Library
The Precincts
Canterbury
CT1 2EH

Contents

A Tschutzkian in armour, with his wife and child
(E. Harding, *The Costume of the Russian empire,* 1803. IFP190)

Travelling through libraries

WHAT is the relation of travel and travel literature, and how can we – as contemporary readers – relate to the travel narratives of the past?

We can begin to approach these questions through examining the text of Valerius, a Galician monk of the seventh century who wrote a letter to his fellow monks in the monastery of El Vierzo in north-western Spain praising Egeria, a pilgrim whose late fourth-century narrative of her journey to the Holy Places is one of the earliest extant pilgrim accounts. Valerius lauds Egeria for taking on 'the labour of travelling the whole world, the perils of seas and rivers, the dread crags and fearsome mountains, [and] the savage menaces of the heathen tribes' (Valerius 1971: 177, 3) in order to bear witness to and pray at sites commemorated in scripture and liturgy.

Whetting the appetites of his fellow monks with descriptions of Egeria's mountain-climbing exploits and of her spiritual ecstasies at being present at 'the most holy places of the birth, passion and resurrection of the Lord, and of the [graves of the] bodies of countless holy martyrs in many different provinces and cities' (Valerius 1971: 175–176, Ib), Valerius ends his account by returning his audience once again to the narrow passages of their cloistered lives:

> ... she gave us an example of following God which is marvellously profitable for many. ... there are many paths to righteousness, but all lead to our single native land, the kingdom of heaven; since also with God's help there remains virtue in labours, in watchings, in fastings, in frequent prayers, and all the observations which go to make up our obedience to our Rule, so we must be ready, and day and night without wearying abstain from all forbidden pleasures, and the snares of this world with its manifold wickedness (Valerius 1971: 178, 4b).

Although Valerius's rhetorical machinations – by means of which he distills Egeria's enthusiastic perambulations into an essence of dedication which he then renders equivalent to the obedience binding a monk to his order's rule – are undoubtedly sincere, the story of Egeria's travels and the zest with which Valerius recounts it (in the course of which inventing a few savage heathens and amplifying the craggy dread of the mountains) leaves a residue of pleasure and excitement which is not consumed by the process of drawing inspiration from the text. In this excess we see something fundamental to travel literature. Travel writing provides vicarious pleasures and experiences to persons unable to follow the footsteps of the voyagers who broach the limits of their readers' lives and bring back words evoking distant and unattainable sights and adventures. Travel literature *stands in for* travel.

Valerius, however, points to another connection between travel literature and travel in cataloguing Egeria's own preparations for her pilgrimage:

> First with great industry she perused all the books of the Old and New Testaments, and discovered all its descriptions of the holy wonders of the world; and its regions, provinces, cities, mountains and deserts. Then in eager haste (though it was to take many years) she set out, with God's help, to explore them (Valerius 1971: 175, 1c).

Travellers, even in times when libraries were neither as extensive nor as prolific as they are today, tend to 'know a field' through other narratives before entering into it in fact. In *Writers and Pilgrims: Medieval Pilgrimage Narratives and their Posterity*, Donald Howard writes that 'travel itself is "imaginative"; travels are fictions to the extent that the traveller sees what he wants or expects to see, which is often what he has read' (Howard 1980: 10). In the late classical period, as in the medieval ages which evolved from it, written material, as well as much of the sanctioned knowledge that passed orally, dealt with the Bible and with texts elaborating biblical materials or themes.

Although Valerius only mentions Egeria's biblical sources, her reference to non-biblical figures such as King Abgar (Egeria 1971: 115–117, xix) suggests her knowledge of the holy places was augmented by extra-biblical materials such as saints' lives and descriptions of the Holy Land by Jerome, Eusebius, the Bordeaux Pilgrim and the like others circulating within the Roman Empire (see Wilkinson 1971: 10–26 and Wilken 1992: 82–125). Burchard of Mount Sion, writing in the thirteenth century, points out that word of the Holy Land permeated every moment of a Christian's life: 'for what hour is there of the day or night all the year round wherein every devout Christian doth not by singing, reading, chanting, preaching and meditating, read what hath been done or written in this land and in its cities and holy places?' (Burchard 1895–1896: 4). In my 'Mapping History's Redemption', I suggest that this may have been the case in the fourth century as well; certainly the Bordeaux Pilgrim's early fourth-century pilgrim narrative is likely to have served as a devotional mnemonic for the catechetical instruction of persons preparing for initiation into the early church (Bowman 1998: 184).

Thus for Egeria, as Leo Spitzer notes in a significant early study of her narrative, the landscape exists as an extension of scripture: 'the eye of the pilgrim wanders incessantly from the Biblical locus (i.e. passage) to the locus (locality) in Palestine' (Spitzer 1949: 239). Egeria's *Travels* (like the *Itinerarium Burdigalense* before it) presents only that part of the world which can exist as a gloss on the biblical text, and as such is an exemplar for the medieval travel writings which would follow. Beazley, writing at the close of the nineteenth century, claimed of Egeria's medieval successors that 'the religious feeling, which drove men from such great distances, closed their senses to much of human life, to most things that lay not exactly in the path of their devotion' (Beazley 1897: 12).[1]

Beazley's criticism of the blinkered perspectives of the medieval period, which serves as a prolegomenon to what he sees as a new empiricism opening in the wake of the 'Dark Ages', is itself somewhat naïve. Certainly one could criticise his position by engaging in ideological readings of the Renaissance and the subsequent openings towards scientism, as Mary Louise Pratt does in *Imperial Eyes: Travel Writing and Transculturation* (Pratt 1992). I would like to be somewhat less historicist and to suggest that there is something in the relation of texts and travels which *always already* (as Jacques Derrida would say) problematizes the possibility of seeing the world as it is rather than as it has been written. This is the way that discourses encountered in the home culture – whether in the library or in the language of everyday life – give shape to the experience of places beyond the bounds of that culture. Valerius, eulogizing Egeria in the Sinai, notes that she follows carefully the path the Israelites took in their forty years of wandering. However whereas they, led by God, did not trust their guide and often wished to turn back to the Egypt they knew, Egeria is presented as possessing a boundless confidence which never falters as she drives onward in quest of holy sites:

> They, many times hearing God's voice, could see his grace going before them by day and night in the pillar of cloud and fire; yet still they doubted, and thought to retrace their steps. But this woman, *once having heard the voice of the gospel*, hastened to the Mount of the Lord, and went, you may be sure, joyfully and without the slightest delay (Valerius 1971: 175-176, 2a – my emphasis).

Here a textually-mediated knowledge of divinity is revealed as more powerful than unmediated experience of the divine; the Israelites hear the voice of God and distrust it whereas Egeria, having 'heard' no more than a textual echo of others' reports of that voice, confidently strides towards Mount Nebo, towards Jerusalem, and onwards towards Ephesus in Asia (Egeria 1971: 122, 23:10). One can argue, of course, that Egeria's confidence in part devolves from the presence

---

[1] Although subsequent work on medieval travel narrative has drawn out nuances in the approaches of different authors and periods (see, for instance, Campbell 1988, Goodman 1997, Ohler 1989 and, for a good introduction to the history of travel and travel writing, Elsner & Rubiés 1999), Beazley's comment is still in large part apt for most if not all medieval travel writing up to the thirteenth century when the Franciscan missions to China began radically to undermine the theological paradigm (see Dawson 1955).

of a well-developed tourist industry, already operative in the late fourth century to bulwark those with the leisure and wealth to travel against the unexpected, dangerous or discomfiting (see Hunt 1982; Hunt 1984).[2] This, however, does not fully explain Egeria's confidence, much less that of the pilgrims who succeeded her over the next millenium and a half when travelling was much more difficult and dangerous. Egeria's confidence is integrally linked to the fact that she knows where she is going, and she knows where she is going because the literal places she is visiting are already re-presentations of *topoi* she has visited in the library. This is evidenced by the fact that her rituals of approaching sites are rituals not of exploration and perception but of recognition. As she reiterates numerous times in the section of her itinerary dealing with the Sinai, she is guided to a site, her guides link the site to a biblical story she knows, the appropriate passage is read from the Bible, and a liturgy is carried out. Thus of the peak of Jebel Musa she notes:

> All there is on the actual summit of the central mountain is the church and the cave of holy Moses. No one lives there. So when the whole passage [*Exodus* 33.22] had been read to us from the Book of Moses (on the very spot!) we made the Offering in the usual way and received Communion (Egeria 1971: 94, 3:5-6).

She staples the landscape to the biblical text through reading the appropriate biblical passage at the designated site and sanctifying the attachment through performing Communion. In this manner she maps the familiar domain on to the foreign landscape, domesticating the latter and asserting its continuity with home. The panic of the children of Israel was, contrarily, a result of their inability to thus map their experiences in terms of preconceived notions. Their experience of the Sinai was far more terrifying than Egeria's. They had been wrenched from their homes and cast into a foreign and barren territory where they witnessed incomprehensible meteorological phenomena, heard anomalous sounds and saw bizarre feats of transformation. What others would later – with hindsight and the help of an explanatory teleological narrative – designate 'miracles' and 'signs', they could only see as indications that the order of nature within which they had

---

[2] Although the Bordeaux Pilgrim benefited from the Roman network of roads, the Palæstina he travelled in 333 CE had not yet been transformed into a 'Holy Land' and hence was without an established itinerary of sites and the accoutrements (guides, pilgrim hospices, authoritative stories) which grow up around them. The development of the Holy Land is a fascinating study in the relation of text and place as many sites were 'invented' in the fourth century (and then again during the period of the Crusader Kingdom) to give place to biblically-grounded names. While some were chosen because of continuities of Jewish or local traditions, and others because of phonemic similarities in names, others were developed because they were close to roads pilgrims already travelled.

build their lives and logics had been torn, releasing spasms of force which might be demonic, might manifest witchcraft, might be the workings of divinity, or might simply be signs that they had strayed into the realms of madness. It is not surprising that the wandering Israelites wanted 'to retrace their steps' so they could walk again on familiar ground. In the Sinai they were not travellers but victims of radical displacement, refugees expelled into a territory they'd never imagined existed. While they did not see the world any more empirically or realistically than did Egeria, she – having mapped out a series of expectations before setting out on her voyage – enjoyed the pleasure of discovering that Arabia and Palæstina were as wonderful as she'd imagined them, while they found themselves thrown into places and events which stretched their home-grown cognitive categories beyond breaking point. They attempted to flee that madness and, when that failed, to impose upon it – through a frenzy of making idols, following charismatic leaders and forging myths – blazes that might lead them back to a comprehensible and controllable world.

I have opened this introduction with a discussion of texts substantially predating those cited in *In Foreign Parts* because I want to suggest two things. The first is that what we see as 'modern' relations of travel writing and travel – the vicarious pleasures of the former and the dependency of the latter on the language and texts of home – have in fact existed as long as travellers relayed stories of their voyages to those at home.[3] The second is that the development of both travel writing and travel depends not on advances in the sophistication of the ways we discern and describe 'the real world' but on shifts in what we look for in our readings both of texts and territories. The volumes pertaining to travel in Canterbury Cathedral Library which have been painstakingly catalogued here by Helen Southwood (with the substantial assistance of Sarah Gray and David Shaw) relate in large part to the post-medieval ages of exploration and of colonisation. As such, the materials they set out were mobilised to increase understanding of the geography of the world beyond the borders of Europe, to catalogue and evaluate the resources (natural, cultural, and human) to be found in those foreign climes, and to assess the cultures found there in terms of the relations that could be had with the peoples who maintained them. In this the texts differ greatly from the pilgrim texts of Egeria and her successors, and the audiences of these are likely to be considerably more catholic in their interests than the likes of the monks who made up Valerius' audience.

---

[3] All of the elements of which I speak in the early Christian materials are implicit as well in the Epic of Gilgamesh (the oldest sections of which date to *ca.* 2000 BCE), and the simultaneity of a radically modern cultural relativism with archaic mythologising in both Xenophanes (sixth c. BCE) and Herodotus (fifth c. BCE) remains striking (and oddly modern).

There are, however, generic similarities which should not be overlooked. For one thing, many if not most of these texts have been and can be read to garner the same pleasure in partaking in others' adventures as were those of the pilgrims. Another thing, perhaps more significant, is that these texts of exploration, colonisation and missionisation were inspirational for their contemporaries in the same way as Egeria's was for the monks of El Vierzo. Cultural tasks may change, but the role played by travel literature in promoting enthusiasm for those tasks has not; Valerius praised Egeria for providing an example of 'the vigour with which we must perform the various tasks which fall to us if we are to obtain the reward of the kingdom of heaven' (Valerius 1971: 174, 1a) while Hakluyt's *The Principall Navigations, Voiages and Discoveries of the English Nation* (1589) is prefaced by his self-ascription as 'publicist and counselor for present and future national enterprises across the ocean' and all the titles of Samuel Purchas's compilations (some of which incorporated Hakluyt's work) refer to pilgrims or pilgrimages, making explicit a continuity between attaining the kingdom of God through pilgrimage and through exploration, conquest and colonisation.[4] The inspiration such texts provide, however, is not directed only to future explorers or colonialists. In the preface to *Eight Years in Ceylon* (1880) the author (Sir Samuel W. Baker, M.A., F.R.S., F.R.G.S.) writes that

> It is not every temperament that is fitted for the anxieties of a wild life in a strange land. This many persons who have left England confident in their own strength have discovered, unfortunately, when too late. Englishmen, however, are naturally endowed with a spirit of adventure. There is in the hearts of all a germ of freedom which longs to break through the barriers that confine us...This innate spirit of action is the mainspring of the power of England (Baker 1880: xiii).

Baker seeks to inspire his audience with tales of dedication and adventure carried out overseas not so much to ensure that it follows in the footsteps of the colonist but in order to impel it to play its part – at home or abroad – in the project of national expansion and glorification it shares with the traveller. Whereas Valerius's collective project is soteriological and Baker's is imperialist, another substantial shift of duty and of community has occurred since the late nineteenth century. An analyst of contemporary travel writing – which overwhelms the shelves of bookshops and floods out of the pages of newspapers into other media such as television – might note a decline in the chauvinism and ideological confidence which had characterised the colonialist and missionary texts of earlier

---

[4] See Purchas, *His Pilgrimage; or, Relations of the World and the Religion Observed in All Ages* (1613), *Purchas, His Pilgrim: Microcosmus, or the Historie of Man* (1613) and *Hakluytus Posthumus or Purchas His Pilgrimes* (1625).

centuries.[5] Modern travel writing nonetheless remains inspirational in evoking foreign places and the cultural objects of other peoples as desirable commodities which we, as dedicated consumers, can aspire to experience and possess. International tourism – very much a late twentieth-century development (Fussell 1980) – is an 'outward-looking' manifestation of the victory of international capitalism in the same way that the conspicuous consumption of ethnic and foreign artifacts is its domestic marker. We – in working so as to travel and consume – play our roles in ensuring the continuance and expansion of that market economy (MacCannell 1976).

To stress the generic continuities in travel writing and its relation to travel is not to deny that travel narratives over time have changed radically both in their contents and in the contexts they address. The capacities of travel writing to provide vicarious pleasure and to evoke in its readers an enthusiastic sense of cultural consanguinity with the traveller are functions, but the material those writings work and rework to provide pleasure and evoke community – as well as the cultural settings in which they operate – have seen substantial transformations over time. Put crudely, the theological paradigm which informed much of travel (and other) writing through the Late Roman and Medieval periods gave way to a naturalism which became positivistic before itself succumbing to the (shallow) cultural relativism informing much contemporary travel writing. Even within those broad categories multiple nuances coexist alongside the occasional work – or series of works – which breaks radically with the dominant paradigm (without necessarily undermining or overturning it). The possibility of taking pleasure from a text written in accordance with an earlier age's paradigm is undermined by these changes, and the identification the text requires us to make with the culture of the traveller is rendered nearly impossible. What gives pleasure in one era is likely to provoke boredom or horror in another, and the community a text calls upon us to recognize as our own might be unrecognisable to someone whose sense of identity and the social has developed in a different period. To sense this one need only attempt to read *Egeria's Travels* the way a contemporary of Valerius might have, or to imagine how a fourth-century Christian might respond to an evocation of the sea, sun, sex and sand milieu of the modern-day Sinai resort of Eilat.

Travel narratives are rhetorical structures which gather materials from writers' experiences or imaginations and link them together so that they pose replies to queries and concerns circulating in the communities they address. They are, in

---

[5] Although certain popular genres of travel writing – particularly those dealing with the Islamic world – construct and maintain strong senses of Western Judæo-Christian community by caricaturising and demonising the 'other' which threatens its borders and its integrity.

other words, particular cultural artefacts. What we experience when we read travel narratives of earlier periods is thus potentially a double displacement; in reading travels we 'go abroad' vicariously, but we also see those foreign shores in the light of projects which we are unlikely to share and through eyes directed by different concerns than our own. Our encounters with the travel writings of previous eras are not unlike the 'encounters with the other' Southwood invokes in her introduction – except that in this case the alterity we encounter is that of our own culture's past. The concerns of empire, the fervour of mission, the *hubris* of Enlightenment superiority organise, in nuanced ways, the structures of perception which give form to travellers' experiences as well as the rhetorics which translate them into text. Of course, it is always possible to ignore this alterity, and thus to miss out on many of the treasures travellers discern in the regions travelled and many of the provocative incongruities evident in the ways they organise their findings for their audiences. We can, like latter-day Egerias, move through travel libraries knowing already what we will find and taking our – rather minimal – pleasures from the confirmation that what we expected is there. We expect to find imperial arrogance, and it is there; we expect to find racialism, and it is rife; we expect an evangelising indifference to the cultural richnesses of other cultures, and of course we can discern the truth marching on and over. To approach the literature in this manner is, however, to miss things not only of great interest but also of great value.

The texts catalogued in this volume offer a particular viewpoint on the development of modernity; as Southwood points out they chronicle the first great encounter of 'the West with the rest' and it is in this encounter that essential blocks of the foundations of the modern world system were laid. These texts elaborate and field-test the systems and theories which are realised in the contemporary empirical sciences, which chronicle the imagining and the realising of imperial systems, which explore the social and cultural systems of other people in order both to record their peculiarities and to assess how to incorporate those people into Western-oriented cultural structures, and which test systems of population control on other peoples which will in turn be applied to the populations of Western Europe.[6] A careful reader will attain a much deeper understanding of the way in which the world in which we live was shaped over the past four hundred years. They will also realise, as they read of travellers testing their own cultural theories and commonplaces against the resistances of other peoples and other places, that assumptions about the previous hegemony of certain modes of thought are overly simplistic. In many cases travellers provided

---

[6] Although much has been written on these topics, I find Pratt 1992, Wolf 1982, Mitchell 1988, and Todorov 1984 useful and provocative.

the case studies which undermined and prompted the overturning of home truths;[7] in others they raised questions about the truths of their own culture which could not – or would not – be answered at home.

There is no question that the books listed in the following pages offer a treasure trove to the historian, but I want, in closing, to return to the pleasure offered to the 'lay' reader by reading the travel books of the past. In examining Valerius's eulogy to Egeria, I set up an opposition between Egeria's pleasure in 're-cognising' that which she came to foreign parts expecting to find and the anxiety felt by the children of Israel when they found themselves in a place where nothing was familiar and much was terrifying. The former is undoubtedly satisfying to the traveller in that it provides an encounter with the 'real' of what was previously only known through its reproduction in texts or pictures viewed at home; the latter, to the contrary, is redolent with madness and radical alienation. Much of what we will come upon in the travel literature of the Canterbury Cathedral Library partakes in the satisfaction of encountering the expected, in part because most travellers knew what they were looking for and in part because the powers which backed most of them made it easy for them to make over what was incongruous into the image of what they wanted to find. Such encounters are, I suggest, interesting to experience and not so interesting to read about. I know of no past travel records which deal convincingly with the spaces of madness and radical alterity, in large part because if someone is able to return to write such an experience up, he or she has already attempted to translate it into the knowable and such translation, which forces into words that for which there are none, stumbles into cliché and commonplace.[8] When language finds it easy to colonize experience, it gives us nothing but a repetition of the known whereas when language comes up against the unspeakable, it stutters and breaks, giving us nothing (or, in falling defensively back behind the walls of cliché, offers us yet another form of silence).

There is, however, median ground, and it is there – I suggest – that travel literature provides an unalloyed pleasure. John Livingston Lowes, in his fascinating study of the sources of Coleridge's *Kubla Khan* and *The Ryme of the*

---

[7] See for a wonderful example of this Diderot's 'Supplement to the Voyage of Bougainville' (Diderot 1963).

[8] Diaries of disasters provide an exception here; one remains haunted by Shackleton's peripheral sightings of a shadowy fourth accompanying his party of three across the frozen wastes of South Georgia in 1916. In fiction Kurtz's 'The horror! The horror!' (Conrad 1925) calls out across the century *The Heart of Darkness* opened, until it finds its answer in the very real death camps of the Nazis and the killing fields of Cambodia and former Yugoslavia. People do travel to these places and tell their tales, but as Giorgio Agamben – most recent in a long line of commentators – points out, language falters in the face of such horrors (Agamben 1999).

Ancient Mariner, refers eloquently to the poetry to be found in the accounts of early maritime explorers:

> this common feature of their language is inseparable from the nature of their undertaking. It is, in a word, the way they have of clothing the very stuff and substance of romance in the homely, direct, and everyday terms of plain matter of fact. There was really little else that they could do. They sailed into regions of the fantastically new, and had words, for the most part, for accustomed things alone. And so the strange assumed perforce the guise of the familiar, and familiar terms took on enchanting connotations through their involuntary commerce with the strange (Lowes 1978: 287).

The surrealism of some of the examples he cites – penguins 'short-legged like a goose ... stand upright like little children in white Aprons, in companies together' (Sir John Narborough, cited in Lowes 1978: 290) or sea-crows 'hovering on the sea ... seem to cover the same with a black carpet of cloth or velvet, coming and going with the sea' (unattributed citation in Lowes 1978: 291) – reach their apogee in Frederic Martens' *The Voyage into Spitzbergen and Greenland* wherein the explorer describes 'Slime-Fishes' 'that in themselves are nothing else but slime':

> the Hat Slime-fish [which] hath a blew Button or Knob, that ... may also be compared unto such a Straw Hat as our Women wear. ... the Rose-like-shaped Slime-fish [which has] seven brown small Threads, like spun Silk, or like unto the Threads that flye in the Air about Autumn [and which] are numerous in the North Sea as Atomes in the Air [and the] Slime-fish like a Cap [which is] divided like unto a Pumpkin into six Ribs [and is] as white as Milk (Martens, cited in Lowes 1978: 81-82).

It is the poetry of these descriptions which catch Lowes' fancy, but I – like my teacher Edwin Ardener, who introduced me to Lowes' work – am as caught by the work of cultural creativity at play here and in other travel narratives. Lowes comments that the mariners 'carried (I suppose like most of us) their known and familiar landscape with them, and they had the trick of catching glimpses of it through the strangest light' (Lowes 1978 : 290) but Ardener unpacks that play of familiarity and alterity into a process of world-extension:

> World-structures are located in physical space, and in real aggregates of human beings. It should not be surprising that the extension of physical space, and of the experience of those beings, produces a genuine extension of the structure, with all its co-ordinates in language and thought (Ardener 1989: 145).

It is this 'stretching' of language and the concepts it carries that fascinates me in travel literature. Travellers, in attempting to relay the hitherto nameless and unknown into terms which render it conceivable without simultaneously dissolving its difference into comfortable familiarity, use metaphor and juxtaposition to distort language to the point where it begins to fray and disintegrate. This happens not only in the description of birds and jellyfish, but also – more subversively – in characterisations of social structures and belief systems previously unknown to the readers of these texts. Here, at the outer limits of the world that language gives us and maintains for us, human beings carry out the creative work of making the unknown habitable. There the new flickers briefly before being rendered part of the familiar. In such work there are great brutalities but also great great beauties, and it is a great pleasure to see – in this bibliography – a new map to these spaces of the wondrous.

Glenn Bowman

Department of Anthropology
University of Kent
August 2000

Bibliography

Agamben, Giorgio. 1999. *Remnants of Auschwitz: the Witness and the Archive* (Homo Sacer III). (trans.) Daniel Heller-Roazen. New York: Zone Books.

Ardener, Edwin. 1989. 'The Voice of Prophecy'. In: *The Voice of Prophecy and Other Essays.* (ed.) Malcolm Chapman Oxford: Blackwell. 134–154.

Baker, Sir Samuel W. 1880. *Eight Years in Ceylon.* London: Longmans, Green and Co.

Beazley, C. Raymond. 1897. *The Dawn of Modern Geography I.* Edinburgh: John Murray.

Bowman, Glenn. 1998. 'Mapping History's Redemption: Eschatology and Topography in the *Itinerarium Burdigalense*'. In: *Jerusalem: Its Sanctity and Centrality to Judaism, Christianity and Islam.* (ed.) Lee Levine. New York and Jerusalem: Continuum Press & Magness Press.

Burchard, of Mt. Sion. 1895–1896. *Itinerary* Vol. XII. (trans.) Aubrey Stewart (Palestine Pilgrims' Text Society Library). London.

Campbell, Mary. 1988. *The Witness and the Other World: Exotic European Travel Writing, 400-1600.* Ithaca: Cornell University Press.

Conrad, Joseph. 1925. 'Heart of Darkness'. In: *Youth: A Narrative and Two Other Stories.* VI . Edinburgh: John Grant. 45–162.

Dawson, Christopher (ed.) 1955. *The Mongol Mission: Narratives and Letters of the Franciscan Missionaries in Mongolia and China in the Thirteenth and Fourteenth Centuries.* New York: Sheed and Ward.

Diderot, Denis. 1963. 'Supplement to the Voyage of Bougainville'. In: *Diderot Interpreter of Nature: Selected Writings.* (trans.) Jean Stewart & Jonathan Kemp. New York: International Publishers. 146–191.

Egeria. 1971. 'Egeria's Travels'. In: *Egeria's Travels.* (ed.) John Wilkinson. London: S.P.C.K. 89–147.

Elsner, Jaš Elsner & Joan-Pau Rubiés. 1999. 'Introduction'. In: *Voyages and Visions: Towards a Cultural History of Travel.* (eds) Jaš Elsner & Joan-Pau Rubiés. London: Reaktion Books. 1–56.

Fussell, Paul. 1980. *Abroad: British Literary Traveling Between the Wars.* New York: Oxford University Press.

Goodman, Jennifer. 1997. *Chivalry and Exploration 1298–1630.* Woodbridge: Boydell and Brewer.

Howard, Donald R. 1980. *Writers and Pilgrims: Medieval Pilgrimage Narratives and their Posterity.* Berkeley: University of California Press.

Hunt, E.D. 1982. *Holy Land Pilgrimage in the Later Roman Empire A.D. 312–460.* Oxford: Clarendon Press.

Hunt, E.D. 1984. 'Travel, Tourism and Piety in the Roman Empire: A Context for the Beginnings of Christian Pilgrimage'. In: *Echos du Monde Classique/Classical Views.* XXVIII. pp. 391–417.

Lowes, John Livingston. 1978 (orig. 1927). *The Road to Xanadu: A Study in the Ways of the Imagination.* London: Picador.

MacCannell, Dean. 1976. *The Tourist: A New Theory of the Leisure Class.* London: Macmillan.

Mitchell, Timothy. 1988. *Colonising Egypt* (Cambridge Middle East Library). Cambridge: Cambridge University Press.

Ohler, Norbert. 1989. *The Medieval Traveller* (trans.) Caroline Hillier. Woodbridge: The Boydell Press.

Pratt, Mary Louise. 1992. *Imperial Eyes: Travel Writing and Transculturation.* London: Routledge.

Spitzer, Leo. 1949. 'The Epic Style of the Pilgrim Aetheria'. In: *Comparative Literature.* I.3. pp. 225–258.

Todorov, Tsvetan. 1984. *The Conquest of America: the Question of the Other.* New York: Harper and Row.

Valerius. 1971. 'The Letter in Praise of the Life of the Most Blessed Egeria written to his Brethren Monks of the Vierzo by Valerius'. In: *Egeria's Travels.* (ed.) John Wilkinson. London: S.P.C.K. 174-178.

Wilken, Robert L. 1992. *The Land Called Holy: Palestine in Christian History and Thought.* New Haven: Yale University Press.

Wilkinson, John (ed.) 1971. *Egeria's Travels.* London: S.P.C.K.

Wolf, Eric. 1982. *Europe and the People without History.* Berkeley: University of California Press.

A caravan of llamas in Peru (Theodore de Bry, *America*. 1590–1624. IFP69)

The Dutch encounter elephants in the East Indies (Johann Theodore de Bry, *India Orientalis*. 1598–1601. IFP68)

Introduction to the Catalogue

THIS bibliography is more than just a list of books on a single theme. In fact, the themes are many and diverse. It is about the theory of travel, the nature of collecting and representations of 'otherness'. Topics range from early printed texts on travel theory, such as *The strange and dangerous voyage of Captaine Thomas James, ... with ... an advice concerning the philosophy of these ... discoueryes* (London: 1633; IFP224), James Howell, *Instructions for forreine travell.* (London, 1642; IFP208), or Baudelot de Dairval's *De l'utilité des voyages*, (Paris, 1686, IFP27),[9] through merchants' accounts on returning from the West Indies (such as Nieuhof, 1703), 18th and 19th-century missionary reports, and many political pamphlets relating to governance in East India Company strongholds. Publications that draw on a host of narratives and illustrations are also included, such as the De Bry volumes, Richard Hakluyt, Samuel Purchas, and the Churchill collections; all are collections in their own rights.

These books have been collated here, to form a coherent body relating to travel beyond Western Europe, especially those in which cross-cultural encounters are represented. This introduction will discuss reasons for this project, sketch its chronological and geographical logic, give a brief introduction to the range and context of the publications listed and provide instructions on how to use the information.

Reasons for the bibliography
The compiling of this list began with a clear objective: to identify books in the Cathedral's collections which would be of use to an anthropologist. It rapidly became obvious that all the Cathedral's rare books are objects that are of use to cultural historians and social scientists. Publications are therefore included here because they demonstrate contact between western Europeans and the 'Other', though this encounter varies dramatically from text to text. The significance of this bibliography to researchers in many disciplines is the fact that the books not only represent 'other cultures' from a western Eurocentric point of view but are

---

[9] Another earlier work is Joseph Hall, *Quo Vadis? A iust censure of travell as it is commonly undertaken by the gentlemen of our nation,* London, 1617 (STC 12705; Mendham H19) which is part of the Mendham Collection on deposit at Canterbury Cathedral Library.

artefacts in their own right. Each publication has a 'social life' of its own – if it could tell its own life story, it would tell of the social and economic contexts it had entered and exited from its research and production, through its initial purchase and consequent lending, re-selling or donation to its current recognition as a rare book in the Cathedral Library. These aspects of each book are crucial to understanding the text and illustrations within – books are cultural material as much as a pipe, figurine, or painting in the Bargrave Cabinet of Curiosities. The travellers, authors (who were not always the same people), collectors of information and drawings, printers, distributors, purchasers and lenders are all agents in the Library's cultural history and development. The books are physical evidence of the social and economic relationships that existed. Even as you read this bibliography, a new set of meanings and exchanges are forming, ones that extend ultimately from an original journey, a conversation or barter between, say, Nieuhof and a Brazilian in the seventeenth century.

I have 're-collected' a set of information, gathering not only texts and pictures that conform to my themes, but also the physical books which have their own life stories. They have, in a sense, been taken out of their previous social contexts and forced into a new one, under the title of this bibliography. For example, the 19th-century MP Sir Robert Harry Inglis collected political pamphlets, many of which were given to him in confidence or were 'printed for private circulation only' scrawled on the title page. Clearly the pamphlets were part of a personal collection with a meaning and significance that is not so manifest when they are part of my recollection.

This bibliography has developed to include pamphlets, texts, books, maps and volumes that contain references to western European contact with the rest of the world. This includes early ethnographic studies of 'other peoples' such as the accounts in the *Journal of the Royal Geographical Society* (1831–1880), or the reports of colonials in Canada and India proposing practical solutions to the problems of colonialism and native rulers, religions and people (see for example *Proposal for forming a society*, 1806). One volume is a catalogue of an exhibition in London of Chinese artefacts (Langdon, William B. 'Ten thousand Chinese things') which I have included because it demonstrates a relationship between the visiting British public and the 'exotic' Chinese culture that they view. The catalogue also includes a section of guide books for the various London panorama shows of the first half of the 19th century.

Geographical and Chronological scope
Medieval and early modern publishing and printing houses were often based in Northern and Western Europe (London, Paris, Amsterdam). By excluding books on travel within these areas, I hope a clear definition of the 'Other' has been established and has given form to the bibliography. For example, I have included David Cranz's *The history of Greenland ...* (1767), but I have not included books on parts of western Europe such as Italy. The map shows more precisely the areas

covered in this bibliography. The decision only to include eastern Europe, far northern Europe (Greenland and the Arctic) and Turkey and Greece, may seem arbitrary but a separate study can be made on the publications about western and northern Europe. There are many publications on Italy, Paris, Britain and other parts of western Europe, such as early guide books, maps and descriptions too numerous to include here. Later publications (such as George Clarke, *Extracts from the Final Report of the Chief Protector of Aborigines in New Zealand* (1846)), although not printed in western Europe, are nonetheless products of western European contact, domination and political influence in a place that still required some description of the original inhabitants of the area. Items published in Calcutta, Canada and New Zealand, have been included where appropriate.

This bibliography draws on books published before 1900 in the Cathedral Library's early printed books collections, excluding collections on deposit such as the Mendham Collection.[10] There is a short introduction on the provenance of the collections. An appendix gives brief details of relevant material in the Archives.

From Compendia to Colonials: Range and Significance of the publications

It is hard to contextualise such a diverse range of books, but the one thing they share is their subjectivity. They were all published by western Europeans on topics distinctly beyond western Europe. When you delve into this bibliography, you will enter into a multitude of dimensions; something will capture your imagination and curiosity. It could be Philip Baldaeus's account of Malabar and Coromandel (1672), which transports you to a world of seamen and adventurers in an expanding naval empire built on the spice trade; or it could be the *Missionary Register* (1816–1854) that re-creates experiences and feelings of Christians in British colonies throughout the world as they encounter different cultures and beliefs in a crusade to convert people.

The argument that connects such extremes of publication is the notion of human contact and social research. Stagl suggests that 'the exploration and the domination of the world are related' (Stagl: 166) and he places travel theory and social research in political and intellectual contexts from the 16th to the 18th centuries. Early travel accounts and theorising on pilgrimage and the more secular 'Grand Tour', developed into and alongside the art of collecting; not only of artefacts from exotic places, but also written information on foreign parts and little known countries. Nicolas de Nicolay published his *Les Navigations*

---

[10] *Catalogue of the Law Society's Mendham Collection lent to the University of Kent at Canterbury and housed in Canterbury Cathedral Library*, completed and edited by Sheila Hingley and David Shaw from the catalogue of Helen Carron and others. London, The Law Society, 1994. cliv + 500p. ISBN 1 85328 265 0. Available from the Cathedral Library.

peregrinations et voyages, faicts en la Turquie ... in 1576, depicting the typical costume of various sections of society in northern Africa and the Near East.

The first compendia of information in written form were extensions of fashionable 'Cabinets of Curiosities'. These had appeared in 16th-century Italy, and allowed the upper classes to display their unusual and exotic artefacts under categories in accordance with the mode of the time. The concept of compendia could be translated into text (Stagl: 1995), and collecting information on foreign parts became a legitimate and popular pursuit, as can be seen from the collections of Canon John Bargrave (1610–1680) in the Archives. Richard Hakluyt first published his massive compendium of 'Navigations' in 1589, bringing stories of English successes at sea into the reach of the book-buying public.

In the 16th and early 17th century, the De Bry family published their collection of accounts from abroad, mainly America, in which they edited and illustrated stories proving the cruelty of Catholic Spaniards on that continent, during a time of religious and political upheaval in western Europe. (Bucher, 1981). Publication of books describing people in foreign parts continued throughout the 18th century and the curiosity about foreign travel drove collectors into the historic past; books in this bibliography include Jan Nieuhof's *Voyages and Travels into Brasil and the East Indies* (1703) as well as the 18th-century printing of the journals of '... two Mohammedan travellers who went to ... [India and China] ... in the 9th century' (Suleiman the Merchant, *Ancient accounts of India and China,* 1733). A fascination with other places and people was fuelled by the expansion of European empires, and missionaries and colonials relied heavily on documentation of the indigenous inhabitants for successful economic and political control (Stagl: 126). Much material was generated for such purposes. Claudius Buchanan wrote about the translation of Christianity into Asian languages in *Christian Researches in Asia* (1812). Written and visual representations of 'the other' continued to grow in importance, and shifted in focus and meaning from the earliest educated gentleman's trip to the Holy Land and western Asia, into the 19th century when efforts to civilise and Christianise the native people of Canada and India were in the forefront of parliamentary debate. The Cathedral Library has a good collection of Bibles and New Testaments translated into a variety of 'exotic' languages, e.g.: Algonquin (1661), Arabic (1727), Eskimo (1827), Ojibwa (1833), Gujurati (1864), Magyar (1873), Japanese and Tamil (1883), Telegu (1884), Fijian (1893).

Later still, anthropology (or the science of understanding people and their societies) emerged from the work of missionaries where it had first taken form, and became a recognised discipline. Missionaries were 'first-hand observers and often active participants in the dynamic process of acculturation that took place' (Dening, 1966: 25 quoted in D. Whiteman, 1985: 296), and their understanding of cultures precedes the traditional anthropology of the early years of the 20th century, which itself ultimately developed into today's modern and post-modern study of people.

It is clear then that the re-collection of publications that I present here is a microcosm of the development of travel literature since the beginning of printing (and before). This compendium has its own unique leaning towards some topics rather than others, due to the interests of the original purchasers, subsequent collectors, donors, librarians and the compilers of this work.

How to use this bibliography

Africa, Asia, the Americas, Eastern Europe, the Arctic, and Australasia are all covered in this selection to some extent. The arrangement is simple. The main body of information is contained in the alphabetical sequence, which makes it easy to find a book by author. The geographical index lists areas of the world which are covered by the collection. To find books relating to, for example, Egypt, look for 'Africa' in the geographical index, then the sub-title 'Egypt' and find the abbreviated list of works relating to this subject with an entry number that matches the main full entry in the alphabetical sequence.

Helen Southwood

Bibliography

Appadurai, A. *The social life of things* (University of Cambridge, 1986).

Bucher, B. *Icon and conquest* (University of Chicago Press, 1981).

Stagl, J. *A history of curiosity: the theory of travel 1550–1800* (Harwood Academic Publishers, 1995).

Whiteman, D. 'Missionary documents and anthropological research'. In: *Missionaries, anthropologists and cultural change* (Dept of Anthropology, College of William and Mary, Williamsburg, Virginia, 1985).

A Pawnee Brave
Son of Old Knife
See Appendix P. 247

A Pawnee brave, son of Old Knife
    (Jedidiah Morse, *A report to the Secretary of War, on Indian affairs*, 1822. IFP310)

In Foreign Parts

Books and pamphlets
on the world beyond Western Europe
in Canterbury Cathedral Library

Abudacnus, Josephus. Historia Jacobitarum, seu Coptorum, in Ægypto, Lybia, Nubia, Æthiopia tota, & parte Cypri Insulae habitantium. *Oxonii: e Theatro Sheldoniano, 1675.* [6], 30p. Wing A154.
On the history of the Coptic church.
Previous owners: Binding with arms of D. Huet, Bp of Avranches. Title-page: library inscription of the Parisian Jesuits. Label of M. Eyries. Bookplates of A.C. Burnell and Benjamin Harrison. IFP1

An Account of the King of Mocha and of his country. *In*: Churchill's *Collection of voyages and travels*, London, 1732, vol. 6, pp.355–357.
Includes descriptions of the inhabitants, customs, climate and produce, together with details of an English doctor and his experience of working for the royal family.

African Civilization Society. Report of the committee of the African Civilization Society to the public meeting of the society ... 1842. *London: published by John Murray, 1842.* 99, [1], cxxxiv, [2]p.; plate; folding map.
Reports on advances in learning African languages, the treatment of disease and medical research, and the savage behaviour of local people, as seen by Europeans. Includes transcripts of letters and speeches. Appendices on the Niger Expedition, 1841. Includes a map of the western coast of Africa, and a list of subscribers. IFP2

African Education Society. Report of the proceedings at the formation of the African Education Society ... Washington ...1829 with an address to the public by the Board of Managers. *Washington: printed by James C. Dunn, 1830.* 16p.
The report outlines the aims and methods of educating the local youth of Africa 'to make constant and untiring inroads on their wrong habits and propensities'. IFP3

Alethes. *See*: **The Edinburgh Reviewer refuted.**

Alexander, William, *Artist*. The costume of China, illustrated in forty-eight coloured engravings. *London: published by William Miller, 1805.* [50] leaves, [2]p.; [50] plates.

Descriptions of people, buildings and aspects of Chinese culture as seen by late 18th-century Europeans, with coloured plates.

Includes a cutting from the *Gentleman's Magazine* on the author, a pencil drawing of William Alexander by Dr. Monroe, and a map of the 'English Ambassador's House in Pekin'. IFP4

Allen, John H. A pictorial tour in the Mediterranean: including Malta – Dalmatia – Turkey – Asia Minor – Grecian Archipelago – Egypt – Nubia – Greece – Ionian Islands – Sicily – Italy – and Spain. *London: Longman, Brown, Green, and Longmans, 1843.* [viii], 96p., ills., plates.

Previous owners: John H. Allen (1843); Stephen Lunn Muller (1843); Alexander Wetherell (1849, donor 1876). IFP5

American Society for Colonizing the Free People of Colour. The thirteenth annual report ... With an appendix. Second edition. *Washington: printed by James C. Dunn, Georgetown, D.C., 1830.* xv, [1], 55, [1]p. IFP6

— The fourteenth annual report ... With an appendix. *Washington: printed by James C. Dunn, Georgetown, D.C., 1831.* xxv, [1], 32p.

With a map of Liberia, dated 1831. IFP7

Amyot, Joseph. Lettre de Pekin, sur le génie de la langue Chinoise, et la nature de leur écriture symbolique, comparée avec celle des anciens Égyptiens: ... *A Bruxelles: chez J. L. de Boubers, 1773.* XXXVIII, '46' [*i.e.* 49], [7]p.; plates.

In response to an article in the Royal Society's *Philosophical Transactions*. IFP8

Anderson, Aeneas. A journal of the forces ... on a secret expedition ... in the Mediterranean and Egypt ... with a particular account of Malta. *London: printed for J. Debrett by Wilson and Co. of the Oriental Press, 1802.* xxvii, [1], 532p.; 9 plates (1 folding); map.

With a large folding map of the harbours of Malta. IFP9

Anderson, Charles. Outlines of a plan ... to regulate and carry on the introduction of Indian laborers at Mauritius ... *London: Nichols, 1840.* 23p.

The plan sets out details of the rations each 'lower class Indian native' will be allowed when being transferred to Mauritius. IFP10

Anglerius, Petrus Martyr. The historie of the West-Indies, containing the actes and adventures of the Spaniards, which have conquered and peopled those countries, inriched with varietie of pleasant relation of the manners, ceremonies, lawes, governments, and warres of the Indians. *London: Andrew Hebb, [1625?].* [5], 318 leaves. STC 651.

Translated by Michael Lok; first published by Hakluyt in Latin. Describes the mixing of Catholicism and native beliefs in local Indian culture and language. IFP11

Anson, George, Admiral. A voyage round the world, in the years MDCCXL, I, II, III, IV. By George Anson, ... sent upon an expedition to the South-Seas. Compiled by Richard Walter, chaplain of his Majesty's ship Centurion, in that expedition. *London: printed for the author; by John and Paul Knapton, 1748.* [34], 417, [3]p.; folding plates; maps.

Previous owner: book plate of James Comerford. IFP12

— — The third edition. *London: printed for John and Paul Knapton, 1748.*

Previous owner: Lee Warly (1748). IFP13

Arabia, seu Arabum vicinarumque gentium Orientalium leges, ritus, sacri et profani mores, instituta et historia. *Amstedami: apud Guiljelmum et Ioannem Blaeu, 1635.* 247p.

By Gabriel Sionita, Joannes Hesronita, C. Richerius, J. Cotovicus and others.
Previous owner: 'St: Hunt'.   IFP14

Archer, Edward Caulfield. A letter to the right honourable Lord John Russell, ... upon the policy of permitting emigration from the continent of India to the Mauritius. *London: Pelham Richardson, 1840.* 32p.
Title-page dedication: 'With the Author's Compliments'.   IFP15

Arrowsmith, Aaron. A map exhibiting all the new discoveries in the interior parts of North America, inscribed ... to the ... Company of ... Hudsons Bay. *London: 1796* .   IFP16

— A map of the United States of North America drawn from a number of critical researches. *London: 1796.*   IFP16A

Arthus, Gothard. India Orientalis. *In*: Johann Theodor de Bry, *India Orientalis*, parts 6–10.

Ashmun, Jehudi. History of the American colony in Liberia, from December 1821 to 1823. Compiled from the authentic records of the colony. *Washington City: printed by Way and Gideon, 1826.* 42p. folding plate; map.
With a map of this part of West-coast Africa. Mentions local tribes (Deys, Queahs, and Gurrahs) involved in the colonisation of Liberia.   IFP17

Asiatic Society. Asiatick researches: or, Transactions of the Society, instituted in Bengal, for inquiring into the history and antiquities, the arts, sciences and literature, of Asia. *Calcutta: printed and sold by Manuel Cantopher, at the Honourable the Company's Printing-Office; and sold at London by P. Elmsly, 1788 [–1839].* 20v.
The Society published journals, reports and experiences, as well as formal documents, illustrations and translations of Sanskrit texts, with maps, on topics covering all parts of Asia, from Greece to India and Tibet.
Dedication on end-paper: 'For The Reverend Charles Forster from his truly grateful & affectionate friend J. Jebb. Sept. 25. 1831'. Book plate of Charles Forster.   IFP18

Auber, Peter (?). *See*: **A Letter to the Right Honorable the Earl of Buckinghamshire.**

Babington, Benjamin. *See*: **Beschi, Costanzo Giuseppe.**

Badger, George Percy. The Nestorians and their rituals: with a narrative of a mission to Mesopotamia and Coordistan in 1842–1844 ... also researches into ... the Syrian Jacobites, Papal Syrians, and Chaldeans, and an inquiry into the religious tenets of the Yezeedees. *London: Joseph Masters, 1852.* 2v. (448, 426p.); plates; 2 maps on cloth at end of vol. 1.
Include illustrations of people and buildings. Frontispiece portrait of 'Sheikh Nâsir, the religious head of the Yeseedees'.
Two copies.   IFP19

Baikov, Fedor Isaakovich *and* **Wagener, Zacharias**. An account of two voyages; the first ... into China. The second ... thro' a great part of the world ... Translated from the High-Dutch. *In*: Churchill's *Collection of voyages and travels*, London, 1732, vol. 2, pp. 489–500.
The first describes the route from Moscow to Peking (1645). The second covers Brazil and the East-Indies (c.1633).

Baird, Robert, *D.D.* The progress and prospects of Christianity in the United States of America; with remarks on the subject of slavery in America; and on the intercourse between British and American churches. Third thousand. *London: Partridge and Oakey,*

3

R. Theobald; Edinburgh, Johnson and Hunter; Dublin, P. Dixon, Hardy, and Sons, [1851]. 72p.   IFP20

Baldaeus, Philippus. A true and exact description of the ... East India coasts of Malabar and Coromandel; as also of the Isle of Ceylon ... Translated from the High Dutch. Amsterdam, 1672. *In*: Churchill's *Collection of voyages and travels*, London, 1732, vol. 3, pp. 502–822.

An account of the conquests of the Portuguese and their expulsion by the Dutch. Observations on the Red Sea coast, the Nile and the Ganges delta. The section on Ceylon covers language, natural history, and religion. The last section is entitled *The idolatry of the East-India pagans*. With maps and illustrations.

Banerjea, Krishna Mohana. Remarks on the speech of the Earl of Ellenborough ... on the Bengal petition against Act XXI of 1850, of the Government of India. By Rev. K.M. Banerjea. *Calcutta: R.C. Lepage & Co., 1853.* [2], 61p.

Controversial pamphlet on the hypocritical and confused policies of the British towards native Indian converts and their political and legal rights, with special reference to inheritance.   IFP21

Banks, *Sir* Joseph. *See*: **Hawkesworth, John**, *An account of the voyages.*

Bannister, John William. Sketches of plans for settling in Upper Canada, a portion of the unemployed labourers of Great Britain and Ireland. Third edition. *London: [Francis Marshall?], 1826.* 39p.

Has detailed table of costs for transportation, erecting a log cabin and starting a farmstead.   IFP22

Baptist Missionary Society. Brief view of the Baptist missions and translations: with specimens of various languages in which the Scriptures are translating at the Mission Press, Serampore. ... Compiled from the printed accounts of the Baptist Missionary Society. *London: printed by J. Haddon. Sold by Button & Son; Gale, Curtis, & Fenner; and Hamilton; Seeley; Gardiner; Hatchard; Dugdale and Keene, Dublin; and Innes, Edinburgh, 1815.* 40p.; 2 plates; folding map.

Facsimiles of Eastern scripts. Map of the Baptist missionary stations.   IFP23

— Periodical accounts relative to the Baptist Missionary Society. *Clipstone: J. W. Morris. Sold by Button, London; and may be had of the Baptist Ministers in most of the principal towns, 1800 [–1817].* 6v.; plates (some folding); music.

Journals, letters and reports from missionaries in India, Africa, and America, writing about the success or failure of spreading Christianity and often supplying interesting anthropological material, such as 'An Indian Song' with music (vol. 1).   IFP24

— Report from the Baptist Missionary Society. *[London?]: [Baptist Missionary Society?], [1821].* 28p.

Report on the activities of the Society in India, Ceylon, Java and the West Indies.   IFP25

— A statement of the Committee of the Baptist Missionary Society. *Shacklewell: printed by T. Rutt, 1807.* 24, [2]p.

Signed Andrew Fuller, Secretary. A history and defence of the Baptist Missions. Two copies.   IFP26

Barbot, Jean. An account of the rise and progress of our trade to Africa, preceding the year 1697 as it was offered in print, to the House of Commons, by the Royal-African-Company, anno, 1709. *In*: Churchill's *Collection of voyages and travels*, London, 1732, vol. 5, pp. 665–68.

Apparently by Barbot, who was agent-general of the Company.

— A description of the coasts of North and South Guinea; and of Ethiopia Inferior, vulgarly called Angola ... containing a geographical, political, and natural history of the ... territories ... their product, inhabitants, manners, languages, trade, wars, policy and religion. With a full account of all the European settlements ... With an appendix; being a general account of the first discoveries of America ... and a geographical, political, and natural history of the Antilles-Islands. *In*: Churchill's *Collection of voyages and travels*, London, 1732, vol. 5, pp.1–664.

With charts, maps and detailed drawings of people, wildlife, buildings etc. Includes a section on vocabulary. The appendix is by Antonio de Herrera Tordesillas.

Baron, Samuel. A description of the Kingdom of Tonqueen by S. Baron a native thereof. [1685–86]. *In*: Churchill's *Collection of voyages and travels*, London, 1732, vol. 6, pp. 1–40.

A 17th-century account of Tonqueen (Vietnam) with maps and plates. Notes 'the most material passages of trade, government, and customs of the country, vice and virtue of the people, at least so far as will content ... a moderate mind and be sufficient for a new commissioner to conduct business by'. Illustrations of ceremonial occasions, rope-dancing, martial exercises, musical instruments, etc.

Baudelot de Dairval, Charles César. De l'utilité des voyages, et de l'avantage que la recherche des antiquitez procure aux sçavans. *Paris: chez Pierre Auboüin et Pierre Emery, 1686.* 2v. (732p.); ill.

Previous owner: Stephen Hunt.   IFP27

Baumgarten, Martin von zu Breitenbach. The travels of Martin Baumgarten ... through Egypt, Arabia, Palestine, and Syria ... giving an account of the situation, nature, monuments, and ruins of those countries ... to which is prefix'd, the life of the author. *In*: Churchill's *Collection of voyages and travels*, London, 1732, vol. 1, pp. 381–452.

The journal of Baumgarten's travels (1507) was published after his death from his own and also his servant's observations. The Life was by C. Donauer. As well as descriptions of the nature and histories of the countries visited, the journal includes a rare description of the Mamalukes. The first English translation from the Latin.

Baynes, Charles Robert. A plea for the Madras judges, upon the charges preferred against them, by J.B. Norton. *Madras: published by J. Higginbotham. Printed at the American Mission Press, 1853.* 82p.

In reply to IFP328.   IFP28

Bebb, John. Two letters: viz. one to the Honorable Court of Directors of the East-India Company ... and one to James Cobb ... from John Bebb ... respecting the eleventh proposition, submitted ... to Parliament. *London: printed for Edmund Lloyd, 1813.* 60p.

Opposes attempts to convert the Indian population. Includes a letter to the Court regarding Christianity in India, from a special meeting of the Committee of the Protestant Society, 1813.   IFP29

Beecham, John. Colonization: being remarks on colonization in general, with an examination of the proposals of the Association which has been formed for colonizing New Zealand. Second edition. *London: Hatchards; Seeleys; Hamilton, Adams, & Co., and John Mason, 1838.* 67p.

Previous owner: 'Robert H. Inglis'. With an autograph letter from Beecham to Inglis.   IFP30

— Remarks upon the latest official documents relating to New Zealand: ... with a notice of a pamphlet by Samuel Hinds ... Second edition. *London: Hatchards; Seeleys; Hamilton, Adams, & Co, and John Mason, 1838. 75p.*

With an inserted printed letter by Beecham. For Hinds, see IFP200.   IFP31

Behader, *Beg.* Narrative of the proceedings of the Provincial Council at Patna, in the suit of Behader Beg against Nadara Begum: ... forming together what is generally called in Bengal the Patna Cause. *[London], [1780?].* 87, [1], 79, [1]p.; folding plates.   IFP32

Beke, Charles Tilstone. Christianity among the Gallas. *London: for the British Magazine, 1848. 8p.*

A discussion of the Gallas of the Upper Nile in North Eastern Africa, describing the impact of an imported religion on indigenous beliefs. Beke describes it as the 'lowest form in which the Christian religion probably exists on the face of the globe'.   IFP33

— An essay on the Nile and its tributaries. *London: William Clowes and Sons, 1847.* [2], 84p.; plate; folding map.

Includes comments on how certain places and rivers are known to Europeans and natives. A map is attached showing the locations in 'the countries south of Abessinia'.

          IFP34

— An essay on the sources of the Nile in the Mountains of the Moon. *[London?]: 1848.* 33p.; plate; folding map.

'Read before the Section of Geology and Physical Geography ... British Association for the Advancement of Science ... Swansea ... 1848 ... printed in the Edinburgh New Philosophical Journal, No. XC ... vol xlv' (tp verso).   IFP35

— On the sources of the Nile; being an attempt to assign the limits of the basin of that river. *London: Richard and John E. Taylor, 1849.* [2], 17p.

Records different perceptions and explanations for the Nile from other cultures. Includes a map, marking the Upper Nile and some of the peoples in the area.   IFP36

Bengal Officer. *See*: **Scott Waring, John**, *Vindication of the Hindoos.*

Benzoni, Girolamo. *See*: **Bry, Theodore de**, *America*, pts 4, 5, 6.

Beschi, Costanzo Giuseppe. The adventures of the Gooroo Paramartan: a tale in the Tamul language accompanied by a translation and vocabulary, together with an analysis of the first story. By Benjamin Babington. *London: J. M. Richardson, 1822.* [6], xii,[2], 243p.

Originally written in Tamil by Father Beschi. Mainly published for its linguistic interest, this story also tells us much about 19th-century fascination with other cultures, in this case, India and the Tamil language groups.

Fly-leaf dedication: 'To Benjamin Harrison Jnr. Esq. With the Author's best regards'.

          IFP37

Bisani, Alessandro. A picturesque tour through part of Europe, Asia, and Africa: containing many new remarks on the present state of society ... with plates after designs by James Stuart ... written by an Italian gentleman. *London: printed by J. Davis; for R. Faulder, 1793.* xiv, 241, [1]p.; folding plates.

Written in letter form, this account contains many references to the people and their lives. The artist, James Stuart, travelled in the Mediterranean, Turkey, Tunisia, Gibraltar and other parts of Europe.   IFP38

Bligh, William. A voyage to the South Sea ... for the purpose of conveying the bread-fruit tree to the West Indies ... in His Majesty's ship the Bounty, commanded by Lieutenant

William Bligh. Including an account of the mutiny ... *London: printed for George Nicol, 1792.* [10], 264p.; folding plates; maps.

With plans and maps relating to Bligh's voyage from the Friendly Islands (Tonga) to Timor, in south-east Asia, and Australasia via the Cape of Good Hope.   IFP39

Blount, *Sir* **Henry.** A voyage into the Levant: a brief relation of a journey lately performed by Mr Henry Blunt gentleman, from England by the way of Venice, into Dalmatia, Sclavonia, Bosna, Hungary, Macedonia, Thessaly, Thrace, Rhodes and Egypt unto Gran Cairo: with particular observations concerning the moderne condition of the Turks and other people under that Empire. The fourth edition. *London: printed by R.C. for Andrew Crooke, 1650.* 228p. Wing B3316.

Previous owner: Lee Warly (1750).   IFP40

Bolland, Richard. A draught of the Streights of Gibraltar with some observations upon the currents thereunto belonging. *In*: Churchill's *Collection of voyages and travels*, London, 1732, vol. 4, pp. 782–84.

Very detailed plan, with tide tables and commentary. Two further plates with diagrams of the sounding boat and the lead used for measuring currents.

Bomanji Dosabhai, *Munshi.* Concise remarks on the principal national governments, together with some suggestions & improvements in the British Indian government, for the benefit of India and the Indians; preparatory to the renewal of the Hon'ble Company's charter ... added to a dissertation on the condition of the kunbi, or Indian peasant by Bomanji Dosabhai Munshi. *Bombay: Telegraph and Courier Press, Shapoorjer Framjee, printer, [1853].* [2], 50p.   IFP41

Bombay briberies; a tale of the present charter. Inscribed to ... Sir Charles Wood. ... By Indus. *London: Effingham Wilson, 1853.* [2], 2, iii–iv, [3]–68p.

Reprinted from the *Daily News*. On Sir James Outram's dismissal from Baroda (see IFP338).   IFP42

Borneo Church Mission Institution. An address of the Committee of the Borneo Church Mission Institution. *[London]: Richards, [1850].* 12p.

Includes correspondence with Sir James Brooke, the Rajah of Sarawak.   IFP43

— Proceedings at a public meeting of the friends of the Borneo Church Mission, held at the Hanover Square Rooms, ... 1847. *London: Richards, printer, 1848.* 25p.

The motion to support the dispatch of two missionaries to Sarawak was proposed by Sir R.H. Inglis.   IFP44

— Report of the Borneo Church Mission Institution, with abstract of receipts and expenditure. *[London]: Richards, printer, [1849, 1851].* 28p.

Reports for 1848 and 1850.   IFP45

Borri, Cristoforo. An account of Cochin-China in two parts. The first treats of the temporal state of that kingdom. The second, of what concerns the spiritual [1620]. *In*: Churchill's *Collection of voyages and travels*, London, 1732, vol. 2, pp. 721–765.

Borri lived for five years among the Chinese and gives an eye-witness description of the country and its inhabitants.

Boulton, Henry John. A short sketch of the Province of Upper Canada for the information of the labouring poor throughout England. To which is prefixed Thoughts on colonization. *London: John Murray, 1826.* 60p.

Endpaper: 'Sir Robt Inglis M.P. with Mr Boultons Compl[imen]ts.'   IFP46

Braid, William David. Statement of the East India Company's conduct towards the Carnatic stipendiaries. *London: Thomas Scott, 1853.* 31, [1]p.
With a glossary of Indian technical terms. IFP47

Brereton, Charles David, *the Younger.* An address, with a proposal for the foundation of a church, mission-house, and school at Sarawak, on the north-west coast of Borneo, under the protection of James Brooke, Esq. *London: Chapman and Hall, 1846.* 35, [1]p.; [3] plates (some folding); maps.
With appendix of extracts by Sir James Brooke, describing the Dyak inhabitants, praising their characters but noting their 'ignorance of all forms of worship and all idea of future responsibility', arguing that a school and church are necessary.
Part of a volume containing pamphlets regarding Brooke and the massacre allegations, including his prosecution. IFP48

Brerewood, Edward. Enquiries touching the diuersity of languages, and religions, through the chiefe parts of the world. *London: printed by Iohn Bill, 1622.* [24], 203, [1]p. STC 3619.
Brerewood discusses languages in eastern Europe, Siberia, Africa and Arabia, recognising the diverse cultures and religions that are represented in different languages. He comments that 'idolatrie spreadeth farthest in America ... at least six parts of seven inhabited with heathenish and idolatrous people'.
Previous owners: Henry Rogers; Henry Oxinden; John Warly (1674); Lee Warly (1740). IFP49

— — *London: Iohn Norton for Ioyce Norton and Richard* Whitaker, *1635.* [24], 203, [1]p. STC 3621.
Two copies. Previous owners: Thomas Dixon; Isaac Reed (1790); Robert Harry Inglis (stamp). IFP50

Brief remarks on the missionary question. *London: printed by W. Pople, 1807.* 16p.
Against John Scott Waring (IFP413) and Twining's proposed resolution to the East India Company against missionary activity (IFP484).
Marked up with MS annotations: possibly a proof copy. Title-page marked '(Not published)'. IFP51

Brief statement of facts relating to the estate of Samuel Troutback, late of Madras, deceased. On behalf of his next of kin, claiming it from the Crown.. *London: W. Clowes, 1836.* 23p; genealogical tables.
Two copies, one with previous owner: 'Robert Harry Inglis.' IFP52

Briet, Philippe. Parallela geographiae veteris et nouae. *Parisiis: sumptibus Sebastiani Cramoisy et Gabrielis Cramoisy, 1648 [–1649].* 2v. (512, 1046p.); folding plates; maps.
With diagrams of the world and continents, useful for past conceptions of geography.
Previous owner: Stephen Hunt. IFP53

British and Foreign Bible Society. Reports of the British and Foreign Bible Society, with extracts of correspondence, &c. *London: printed for the Society, by J. Tilling; sold by L.B. Seeley; J. Hatchard; Oliphant, Waugh, and Innes, Edinburgh, 1805–1851.* 29v.
Reports, letters, and correspondence between missionaries in all parts of the world, relevant for the study of the growth and impact of Christianity in the 19th century and the way other cultures received the new religion. Volume one includes a list of Bibles in various languages in the library of the Society. IFP54

British India Association of Bengal. Desiderata for British India, as communicated by Baboo Prosonno Comar Tagore, a member of the British Indian Association of Bengal. *[London]: [1852].* 12p.; mauve wrapper.   IFP55

— Rules of the British India Association. Established 29th October, 1851. *London: Re-printed by Hunt & Son, 1852.* 8p.
'The Association is composed entirely of natives, and is altogether free from European influence.' — Originally published in Calcutta.   IFP56

British opium trade with China (from the *Leeds Mercury* of September 7th 1839). *Birmingham: B. Hudson, printer, [1839?].* 28p.   IFP57

Bromley, Walter. An account of the aborigines of Nova Scotia called the Micmac Indians. *London: printed by Luke Hansard & Sons, 1822.* 11, [1]p.
Bromley was Superintendent of the Lancasteran or Royal Acadian Institution in Halifax, Nova Scotia. Includes a list of articles imported from Nova Scotia free of duty.   IFP58

— An appeal to the virtue and good sense of the inhabitants of Great Britain, &c. in behalf of the Indians of North America. *Halifax [Nova Scotia]: printed by Edmund Ward, 1820.* 57, [1]p.
Bromley argues against the British treatment of the indigenous people of North America: 'What authority have we to become the general possessors of the Indian territory, to the total exclusion of its original possessors?' (p.5). With a table of the present and imperfect tenses in Micmac by Peter Duponceau.   IFP59

Brooke, *Sir* James, *Rajah of Sarawak*. A letter from Borneo; with notices of the country and its inhabitants. Addressed to James Gardner, Esq. *London: published by L. and G. Seeley; and sold by Smith, Elder, & Co., 1842.* 40p.; folding plate; map.
Mentions the value Borneo would have to Britain through commercial activity, in spite of the high prices demanded by the Dyaks. Describes the Dyaks' lives and produce, and proposes a policy of cultural contact with the different chiefs 'by visiting them once or twice a year, and inspiring a confidence in our good intentions' (p. 33). The map shows the settlements on the north-west coast of Borneo.   IFP60

— A vindication of his character and proceedings in reply to the statements privately printed and circulated by Joseph Hume, ... by Sir James Brooke. *London: James Ridgway, 1853.* 64p.   IFP61

— *See also*: **Borneo Church Mission Institution**; **Brereton, Charles David**; **Report of the proceedings**.

Broughton, Thomas. An historical dictionary of all religions from the creation of the world to this present time. *London: printed for C. Davis and T. Harris, 1742.* 2v. (606, 563p.); plate.
Definitions of many religions and their attributes, from the ancient Greeks and Romans to contemporary Jews and Muslims, and beliefs from other parts of the world, for example Bensaiten, the Japanese goddess of riches.
Previous owner: Lee Warly (1750).   IFP62

Brouwer, Hendrik *and* Herckmans, Elias. A voyage to the kingdom of Chili in America ... in the years 1642 and 1643. With a description of the Isle of Formosa and Japan. Translated from the High-Dutch, printed at Frankford upon the Maine, 1649. *In*: Churchill's *Collection of voyages and travels*, London, 1732, vol. 1, pp. 453–485.
Brouwer and Herckmans were sent to Chile by the Dutch West-India Company. Includes an account of the voyage and a description of the island of Castro off the south coast of

Chile, and the Valdivia river. The accounts of Formosa (Taiwan) and Japan are by Georgius Candidius.

Browne, Edward. A brief account of some travels in Hungaria, Servia, Bulgaria, Macedonia, Thessaly, Austria, Styria, Carinthia, Carniola and Friuli. *London: printed by T.R. for Benj. Tooke, 1673.* [12], 144, [4]p.; plates (some folding). Wing B5110.
Brown, son of Sir Thomas Brown, was Physician in Ordinary to Charles II. A personal record of his journey, with plates and drawings.   IFP63

Bruce, James. Travels to discover the source of the Nile, in the years 1768 ... 1773. *Edinburgh: printed by J. Ruthven, for G. G. J. and J. Robinson, London, 1790.* 4v.; plates.
This account, though the result of clear geographical and historical objectives, includes interesting details of the travellers' encounters with new people and cultures. For Murray's *Life* of Bruce, see IFP316.   IFP64

—— — The second edition. *Edinburgh: printed by James Ballantyne, for Archibald Constable and Co., and Manners and Miller; and Longman, Hurst, Rees and Orme, London, 1805.* 8v.; plates; maps.   IFP65

Bruce, John, *M.P.* Historical view of plans, for the government of British India, and regulation of trade to the East Indies. And outlines of a plan of foreign government, of commercial œconomy, and of domestic administration, for the Asiatic interests of Great Britain. *[London]: [privately printed], 1793.* xii, 632, [2]p.
This colonial history discusses the political and financial advantages and consequences of British trade, law and administration in India.   IFP66

Bruin, Cornelis de. Travels into Muscovy, Persia, and part of the East-Indies. Containing an accurate description of whatever is most remarkable in those countries. ... with above 320 copper plates ... To which is added, an account of the journey of Mr. Isbrants ... to China. *London: for A. Bettesworth and C. Hitch, S. Birt, C. Davis, J. Clarke, S. Harding, D. Browne, A. Millar, J. Shuckburgh, and T. Osborne, 1737.* 2v. (244, 223p.); plates (some folding).
The author's account of his travels in the early 1700s, with descriptions of the people he met and their everyday lives. With maps and many plates depicting towns and people. The work includes accounts by John Chardin.
Previous owners: John Page, Elham; Lee Warly (1750).   IFP67

Bry, Johann Theodore de. India Orientalis. *Francofurti: Excudebat VVolffgangus Richter, impensis Io. Theo. & Io. Israel. de Bry, 1598–1601.* In 12 parts.
Johann Theodore de Bry and Israel de Bry succeeded their father Theodore as publishers of collections of accounts of travels mostly to America and to the East Indies. These were the first illustrated texts on the Americas made available to Europeans, utilising a variety of sources: journals, ship's logs, and previously published material used by Richard Hakluyt. Authors or compilers of the individual parts include Gothard Arthus, Pedro Fernandes de Queiros, Jan Huygen van Linschoten, Duarte Lopes, Filippo Pigafetta, Bilibaldus Strobaeus, Amerigo Vespucci.   IFP68

Part 1: Regnum Congo hoc est vera descriptio Regni Africani, quod ... Congus appellatur. Per Philippum Pigafettam, olim ex Edoardi Lopez acroamatis lingua Italica excerpta.
Part 2: Iohan. Hugonis Lintscotani Nauigatio in Orientem, item regna ... moresque Indorum & Lusitanorum pariter in Oriente degentium: ... Ea Lintscotus ... primùm ...

Belgice in publicum dedit: ... nunc ... Latine ... reddita enunciauit Teucrides Annaeus Lonicerus ... Additae sunt ... D. Paludani annotationes.

Part 3: Secunda pars nauigationum à Ioanne Hugone Lintschotano ... in Orientem susceptarum; ... Nauigatio Hollandorum in insulas Orientales, Iauan & Sumatram: ... Tres nauigationes Hollandorum in ... Indiam per Septentrionalem ... Oceanum ... de Germanico in Latinum translata ... à Bilibaldo Strobaeo.

Part 4: Primum varij generis animalia, fructus, arbores: ... ac gemmarum species pleraque, sicut in India tum effodiantur, tum generentur; ... describuntur. Per Ioannem Hugonem Lintschotanum, & nonnullos alios. Descriptioni huic adiectae, ... sunt annotationes ... Bernhardi Paludani ... Secundo: nouissima Hollandorum in Indiam Orientalem nauigatio ... 1598. ... 1599. .... exponitur. Omnia ex Germanico Latinitate donata, studio & opera Bilibaldi Strobaei.

Part 5: Descriptio vniuersae nauigationis illius, quam Hollandi ... in terras Orientales, praecipuè verò in Iauanas & Moluccanas insulas, Bantam, Bandam & Ternatem, &c. susceperunt: ... Opus Belgica lingua primò editum: ... & ... iam Latio donatum à Bilibaldo Strobaeo.

Part 6: Veram et historicam descriptionem auriferi regni Guineae, ad Africam pertinentis, quod alias Littus de Mina vocant, continens, ... Latinitate ex Germanico donata studio & opera M. Gotardi Arthus ... illustrata ...

Part 7: Nauigationes duas, primam, trium annorum, à Georgio Spilbergio ... ann. 1601. ex Selandia in Indiam Orientalem susceptam: alteram, nouem annorum, à Casparo Balby ... anno 1579. ex Alepo Babyloniam versus, & inde porro ad regnum Pegu vsque continuatam, continens ... Auctore M. Gotardo Arthus.

Part 8: Nauigationes quinque, ... à Iacobo Neccio, ... Ioanne Hermanno de Bree, ... Cornelio Nicolai, ... Cornelio de Vena, ... Stephano de Hagen ... in Indiam Orientalem susceptas & peractas continens ... Auctore ... Gotardo Arthus.

Part 9: Historicam descriptionem nauigationis ab Hollandis & Selandis in Indiam Orientalem, sub imperio Petri-Guilielmi Verhuffii, ... annis 1607 ... 1609. susceptae ...continens: addita omnium, quae hoc tempore eis obtigerunt, annotatione; auctore ... Gotardo Arthusio.

Part 10: Historica relatio siue descriptio noui ad Aquilonem transitus, supra terras Americanas in Chinam atque Iaponem ducturi, quemadmodum is ab Henrico Hudsono ... nuper inuentus est, addita ... insularum & locorum ... in itinere isto occurrentium, ex Iohannis-Hugonis Lintschottani itinerario desumpta commemoratione. Item discursus ... super detecta nuper quinta orbis parte, Terra ... Australi ... à ... Petro-Ferdinando de Quir, &c. conscriptus. Addita descriptione regionum Siberiae, ... Auctore ... Gotardo Arthusio ...

Part 11: Duarum navigationum, ... in Indiam Orientalem ... 1501. Dn. Americus Vesputius instituit, historia. ... Vera ... Angli cujusdam relatio, ... in extremam Indiae Orientalis oram ... Descriptio regionis Spitzbergae: ... Nunc primum latio donata.

Part 12: Descriptiones ... regnorum, ... illius continentis, quae vulgo Orientalis Indiae nomine censetur: ... Narrationes ... aliquot nauigationum ab Anglis Batauisque ... in ... Orientis & Austri partes susceptarum, ... quibus accessit Periplus orbis terrae, à Iacobo Eremita, ... absolutus.

Bry, Theodore de. America. *Francoforti ad Moenum: typis Ioannis Wecheli, sumtibus Theodore de Bry venales reperiuntur in officina Sigismundi Feirabendi, 1590-1624.* In 12 parts.

Theodore de Bry was an exiled Protestant living in Frankfurt: his work exhibits an anti-Catholic bias in the texts and pictures. Compilers of the individual parts include Girolamo Benzoni, Ulrich Faber, Thomas Harriot, Antonio de Herrera, Jacques Le Moyne de Morgues, Jean de Lery, Joannes Stadius.   IFP69

Part 1: Admiranda narratio fida tamen, de commodis et incolarum ritibus Virginiae, nuper admodum ab Anglis, qui à Dn. Richard Greinvile equestris ... M.D.LXXXV. deducti sunt inventae ... Anglico scripta sermone a Thoma Hariot ... nunc ... Latio donata à C.C.A.

Part 2: Breuis narratio eorum quae in Florida Americae prouincia Gallis acciderunt, secunda in illam nauigatione, duce Renato de Laudonniere ... anno MDLXIIII. Quae est secunda pars Americae ... auctore Iacobo le Moyne, cui cognomen de Morgues, ... primùm Gallico sermone ... edita.

Part 3: Memorabilem provinciae Brasiliae historiam continens, germanico primum sermone scriptam à Ioanne Stadio ... nunc autem latinitate donatam à Teucrio Annaeo Priuato Colchanthe ... Addita est narratio profectionis Ioannis Lerij in eamdem Provinciam.

Part 4: Insignis & admiranda historia de reperta primùm Occidentali India à Christophoro Columbo ... Scripta ab Hieronymo Bezono.

Part 5: Hieronymi Benzoni ... secundae sectionis Hia: Hispanorum, tùm in Nigrittas ... tum in Indos crudelitatem, Gallorumque piratarum de Hispanis toties reportata spolia.

Part 6: Historiae ab Hieronymo Benzono ... scriptae, sectio tertia ... In hac ... reperies, qua ratione Hispani ... Peruani regni prouincias occuparint, capto rege Atabaliba: additus est ... de Fortunatis insulis commentariolus.

Parts 7 and 8: Verissima et iucundissima descriptio praecipuarum quarundam Indiae regionum & insularum, quae ... ab Vlrico Fabro ... multo cum periculo inuentae ... ex germanico in latinum sermonem conuersa autore M. Gotardo Artus.

Part 9: De ratione elementorum: de Noui Orbis natura: ... His accessit designatio illius nauigationis, quam 5. naues Hollandicae anno 1598. per fretum Magellanum tentarunt: quomodo ... Sebalt de Weert ... an. 1600. domum reuersus sit. Addita est tertio nauigatio recens, quam ... Oleuier à Noort ... suscepit: Omnia è Germanico Latinitate donata.

Part 12: Descriptio Indiae Occidentalis, auctore Antonio de Herrera ... Accesserunt et aliorum Indiae Occidentalis descriptiones ... Quibus cohaerent Paralipomena Americae.

Bryce, George. Manitoba: its infancy, growth, and present condition. *London: Sampson, Low, Marston, Searle, & Rivington, 1882.* viii, 367p.

The author was professor at Manitoba College, Winnipeg.   IFP70

Brydges, Harford Jones. The Ameers of Scinde. A letter to ... the Court of Directors of the East India Company. *London: Smith, Elder & Co.; John Wilson, 1843.* 36p.

Criticises the British Government's dealings with the deposed Rajah of Sattara and the Ameers of Scinde; the breaking of treaties and unfair trials which he predicts will bring wars between the two cultures.

Title-page dedication: 'To Sir Robert Harry Inglis Bart From his affectionate friend the Author'.   IFP71

— Case of the Rajah of Satara. Letter to the ... Court of Directors of the East India Company. *London: printed by John Wilson, 1843.* 15p.

Dedication on half-title: 'Sir Robert Harry Inglis B'. M.P. from the Author with his sincere and affectionate Regards. 8 Sept: 1843'. IFP72

— Substance of a speech partly delivered at the India House on Friday July 26, 1833 ... A petition to the ... Commons against the India Bill. *London: James Bohn, 1833.* 31, [1]p.
IFP73

Brydone, Patrick. A tour through Sicily and Malta. In a series of letters to William Beckford, Esq. ... The third edition. *London: printed for W. Strahan; and T. Cadell, 1774.* 2v. (373, 355p.); maps. IFP74

Buchanan, Claudius. Christian researches in Asia: with notices of the translation of the Scriptures into the oriental languages. *Cambridge: printed by J. Smith; and sold by J. Deighton; and Cadell and Davies, London, 1811.* [4], 270p. IFP75

— Christian researches in Asia. To which are prefixed, Two discourses preached before the University of Cambridge. The eighth edition. *London: T. Cadell and W. Davies, 1812.* [4], 314p.
How Christianity is translated into other languages, showing the clashes and overlaps in belief and culture. Useful for studies in vernacular Christianity.
Large-paper copy. Book plate of Archbishop Howley. IFP76

— Review of "A vindication of the Hindoos, by a Bengal officer;" with an appendix, containing a review of remarks on the Christian Observer. *[London?]: Extracted from the Christian Observer, Feb. 1808.* 27p.
A discussion of the appropriateness of introducing Christianity to Indian society, where other beliefs already exist. The 'Bengal officer' is John Scott Waring (IFP417). IFP77

Burckhardt, John Lewis. Notes on the Bedouins and Wahábys, collected during his travels in the East, by the late John Lewis Burckhardt. Published by authority of the Association for Promoting the Discovery of the Interior of Africa. *London: Henry Colburn and Richard Bentley, 1830.* [2], ix, [1], 439, [1]p.; plate; map.
With MS annotations by the Rev. Charles Forster. IFP78

Calcutta Auxiliary Bible Society. The Bible in India. *London: W. H. Dalton, 1853.* 55, [1]p.
Extracted from the Fortieth Report.
Previous owner: 'Robert Harry Inglis 21 April 1853'. IFP79

Campbell, *Sir* George. A scheme for the government of India. *London: John Murray, 1853.* iv, 150, [1]p.; [2] plates; maps.
Reveals the interaction and power relations between the British and the native Indians, with a chapter on 'Share of natives in government'. Map of the Indian jurisdiction on the title-page. IFP80

Candid thoughts, respectfully submitted to the proprietors of East India stock; occasioned by "Mr Twining's letter to the Chairman", and "Observations on the present state of the Company." *[London]: J. Hatchard, J. Butterworth; Blacks, Parry, and Kingsbury, [1807].* 4p.
Signed 'A Christian'. Against Thomas Twining's *Letter* (IFP484) and John Scott Waring's *Observations* (IFP413). IFP81

Carrington, Frederick Augustus. The New Zealand Company. Letter addressed to the Rt. Hon. Viscount Howick chairman of the select committee on New Zealand. Shewing the nature of the land purchases of the Company, and its dealings with the natives and the public ... *London: printed by A. Hancock, 1845.* 36p.

The author defends himself against charges of fraud.

With an autograph letter from the author to Sir R.H. Inglis, dated 6 June 1845. IFP82

Casas, Bartolomé de las. Narratio regionum Indicarum per Hispanos quosdam devastatarum verissima: per episcopum Bartholomaeum Casaum, natione Hispanum Hispanicè conscripta, & Hispali Hispanicè, post alibi Latinè excusa ... *Oppenhemii: sumtibus Johan-Theod. de Bry, typis Hieronymi Galleri, 1614.* 138p.; ill.

With engravings by J.T. and J.I. De Bry after drawings by Jodocus a Winghe, showing the torture of the Indians by the Spanish colonisers. IFP83

The Case of Mr. J. W. Huskisson. *[London?], [1840].* 48p.

Defends John William Huskisson against various personal charges incurred while agent for the Eastern Province of Ceylon. IFP84

Chamerovzow, Louis Alexis. Borneo facts versus Borneo fallacies. An inquiry into the alleged piracies of the Dyaks of Serebas and Sakarran. *[London]: Charles Gilpin, [1851].* 64p.

Accuses Sir James Brooke of committing atrocities in Borneo. IFP85

Chapman, John. Baroda and Bombay; their political morality. *London: John Chapman, 1853.* 174p.

Bribery and corruption amongst the officials in Bombay and Baroda. Concerns the removal of Lieut. Col. Outram (see IFP338) IFP86

— Principles of Indian reform ... Together with a plan for the improvement of the constituency of the East India Company, and for the promotion of Indian public works. *London: John Chapman, 1853.* 36p.

Previous owner: 'Robert Harry Inglis 29 April 1853'. IFP87

Chardin, *Sir* John. Voyages du chevalier Chardin, en Perse, et autres lieux de l'Orient, enrichis d'un grand nombre de belles figures en taille-douce, représentant les antiquités et les choses remarquables du pays. Nouvelle édition. *Paris: de l'imprimerie de Le Normant, 1811.* 11v.; maps.

Contains maps, plates and descriptions of the towns and peoples Chardin encountered during his travels in the seventeenth century. IFP88

— *See also*: **Bruin, Cornelis de**, *Travels into Muscovy.*

Chinese treatise on the vaccine. Originally printed at Canton, in 1805, now lithographed in London, in 1828, by W. Day. *[London]: [W. Day], 1828.* [16]p.; ill.

Entirely in Chinese characters apart from the title-page. IFP89

Church Missionary Society. The case of Archdeacon Henry Williams, in reply to a statement by the Rev. E.G. Marsh. *[Not published]: [1851].* 24p.

On the dispute over the land owned by New Zealand missionaries, in reply to IFP285. Signed by H. Venn and H. Straith. Printed at the top of page 1: 'Confidential'. IFP90

— Letters from the Bishop of New Zealand and Governor Grey, in reference to the large land claims of the missionaries in New Zealand. *[Not published]: [1848].* 16p.

Printed at the top of page 1: 'Confidential'. IFP91

— Missionary register ... containing the principal transactions of the various institutions for propagating the gospel: with the proceedings, at large, of the Church Missionary Society. *London: L.B. Seeley and J. Hatchard, 1816–1854.* 43v.; lacks 1813–1815 and 1855.

Up-to-date reports of missionary activities throughout the world, from West Africa to New Zealand, and South India to South America. Some correspondence and articles contain plates and maps. IFP92

— Report of the Medical Committee, ... of the Church Missionary Society, to examine into the nature and extent of the mortality that has ... prevailed amongst their residents on the western coast of Africa. *London: printed by Ellerton and Henderson, 1825.* 23p.   IFP93

— Statement of the Committee of the Church Missionary Society, in reference to land purchased by the missionaries in New Zealand. *London: Church Missionary Society, 1845.* 19p.

A defence against the charges of land speculation against the missionaries.   IFP94

— *See also*: **Coates, Dandeson; Kempthorne, Sampson.**

Churchill, Awnsham and **John.** A collection of voyages and travels, some now first printed from original manuscripts, others now first published in English. ... With ... an Account of the progress of navigation, from its first beginning. *London: Printed by assignment from Messrs. Churchill. For John Walthoe; Tho. Wotton; Samuel Birt; Daniel Browne; Thomas Osborn; John Shuckburgh; and Henry Lintot, 1732.* 6v., plates (some folding); ill.; maps.

Compiled for the booksellers, Awnsham and John Churchill. The *History of navigation* ascribed to John Locke (BM). Subscription list in vol 1. The individual parts of the collection are given separate entries here under their respective authors.   IFP95

Claim of the Southern Detachment of the Army to prize-money for the taking of Seringapatam. *London: printed by A. Wilson, 1800.* [2], 43p.   IFP96

Clarke, George. Extracts from the final report of the Chief Protector of Aborigines in New Zealand. *[not published]: 1846.* 15p.

Signed 'George Clarke, Chief Protector of Aborigines'. Condemns attempts to evade the terms of the Treaty of Waitangi.

Previous owner: 'Robert Harry Inglis'.   IFP97

Coates, Dandeson. Memoranda and information, for the use of the deputation to Lord Stanley, in reference to the New Zealand mission of the Church Missionary Society. *[Not published]: 1843.* 32p.

Title-page marked 'Confidential'. Prelims signed D. Coates. Contains letters and notes such as a translation of a deed of trust from the natives to the colonisers regarding a piece of land.

Two copies.   IFP98

— The New Zealanders and their lands. The Report of the Select Committee of the House of Commons on New Zealand, considered in a letter to Lord Stanley ... Third edition. *London: Hatchards, Seeleys, Nisbet and Co., 1845.* 72p.

A discussion of the land rights of the native New Zealanders and the Treaty of Waitangi, revealing the attitude of the colonisers to the land and people they 'discovered'.   IFP99

— Notes for the information of those members of the deputation to Lord Glenelg, respecting the New-Zealand Association, who have not attended the meetings of the committee on the subject. *London: printed by Richard Watts, [1837].* 24p.

Signed at end 'D. Coates, Dec. 28th, 1837'. Title-page headed 'Confidential'. Notes and resolutions regarding the colonisation and missionary work in New Zealand, including the rights and well-being of the indigenous Maori peoples.

Two copies.   IFP100

— The principles, objects, and plan of the New-Zealand Association examined, in a letter to the Right Hon. Lord Glenelg, Secretary of State for the Colonies. *London: Hatchards; Seeleys; and Hamilton, Adams and Co., 1837.* 44p.

Remarks on the virtues of civilising the indigenous peoples, for example 'Without police ... the Natives have none of the methods of preventing or punishing crime which are in use in the civilised world' (p.30). IFP101

Cockburn, Sir William, *Dean of York.* A letter to the editors of the Edinburgh Review. *Cambridge: printed at the University Press; and sold by Deighton, Cambridge; Hatchard, London; and Maners and Millar, Edinburgh, 1805.* 16p.
Defends his dissertation on 'the best means of civilizing the subjects of the British Empire in India', which had been unfavourably reviewed by Robert Grant. IFP102

Colden, Cadwallader. The history of the five Indian nations of Canada, which are dependent on the province of New-York in America, and are the barrier between the English and the French in that part of the world ... *London: printed for T. Osborne, 1747.* xvi, [4], 90, [4], 91-204, 283, [1]p.; folding plate; map.
A study of the various Indian nations in North America, with official state papers and treaties. IFP103

— — The third edition. *London: printed for Lockyer Davis; J. Wren; and J. Ward, 1755.* 2v. IFP104

Collier, Jeremy. The great historical, geographical, genealogical and poetical dictionary; being a curious miscellany of sacred and prophane history, containing ... the description ... the religions, government, morals and customs of the inhabitants ... collected from the best historians, chronologers, and lexicographers ... *London: printed for Henry Rhodes, Thomas Newborough, the assigns of L. Meredith; and Elizabeth Harris, 1701.* 2v.; frontispiece. IFP105

Colombo, Fernando. The history of the life and actions of ... Christopher Columbus and of his discovery of the West-Indies call'd the New World ... written by his own son D. Ferdinand Columbus. *In:* Churchill's *Collection of voyages and travels,* London, 1732, vol. 2, pp. 501–628.
Detailed account of the discovery, together with descriptions of the inhabitants, including the Amazons.

The Colonial Church Chronicle, and Missionary Journal. *London: Francis and John Rivington; J.H. Parker, Oxford; J. & J.J. Deighton, Cambridge, 1848–1874.* Vols. 1–27.
Has many articles which illustrate the penetration of European culture into the various territories of the British Empire. IFP106

Common sense. *See:* **Free trade with India.**

Conder, Josiah. Egypt, Nubia and Abyssinia. *London: James Duncan, 1831.* 2v. (366, 364p); [8] plates; [2] folding maps.
Geographical and architectural histories of north-east Africa, with interesting 'ethnographic' chapters such as *Description of the Egyptian Arabs* (vol. 1) and *The origin and physical character of the various tribes of Nubia* (vol. 2). IFP107

Connor, James. *See:* **Jowett, William,** *Christian researches in the Mediterranean.*

Cook, James. A voyage to the Pacific Ocean ... in his Majesty's ships, the Resolution and Discovery. In the years 1776, 1777, 1778, 1779 and 1780 ... with a great variety of portraits of persons ... *London: printed by W. and A. Strahan: for G. Nicol; and T. Cadell, 1784.* 3v. (421, 549, 558p.); plates (some folding); maps.
Cook travelled from Plymouth to the Canary Isles, Mesoamerica, South Africa, Australia and parts of the Pacific Isles such as modern Tahiti, and the Tongas; after a long period here, he went to North America, and returned home via Kamchatka and Indonesia. Rich

anthropological material from a mainly geographical expedition: evidence of 18th-century Western perceptions of the inhabitants' dress, dance, language, property, and lives, from diverse areas of the Pacific. The illustrations are mostly of people and include both 'natives' and Cook's crew.

With a second copy of the atlas volume. IFP108

— — The second edition. *London: Printed by H. Hughs, for G. Nicol, and T. Cadell, 1785.* 3v. (421, 548, 556p.); plates (most fold.); & plate vol.; maps.

Title-page inscription: 'Library of the Church of Canterbury'. IFP109

Cooke, John. *See*: **Montagu, John**, *A voyage.*

Cooley, William Desborough. The Negroland of the Arabs examined and explained; or, an inquiry into the early history and geography of Central Africa. *London: printed by James Holmes. Published by J. Arrowsmith, 1841.* xvi, 143p.; folding plate; map.

Discusses accounts of Ibn Battuta and Ibn Khaldun.

Previous owner: T. Brockman, Sandwich. IFP110

Coote, *Sir* Eyre. A letter from certain gentlemen of the council at Bengal, to the honourable the Secret Committee for affairs of the honourable united Company of Merchants of England trading to the East Indies. Containing reasons against the revolution in favour of Meir Cossim Aly Chan ... brought about by Governor Vansittart ... *London: printed for T. Becket and P. A. de Hondt, 1764.* [2], 25, [1]p.

Signed by Eyre Coote and others. IFP111

Coryate, Thomas. Thomas Coriate traveller for the English wits: greeting. From the court of the Great Mogul, resident at the towne of Asmere, in Easterne India. *[London]: printed by W. Iaggard, and Henry Featherston, 1616.* [6], 56p.; ill.

An account of Coryate's journey to and from India. This edition is apparently an 18th-century type-facsimile of the original (STC 5811). IFP112

Courtenay, Thomas Peregrine. Canada. *London: C. Roworth and Sons, [1838].* 32p.

From the *Foreign Quarterly Review*, April 1838.

Title-page dedication: 'Sir Robert H. Inglis Bart from the Author'. IFP113

Cranz, David. The history of Greenland: containing a description of the country, and its inhabitants ... a relation of the mission ... by the Unitas Fratrum, at New Herrnhuth & Lichtenfels. ... translated from the High-Dutch. *London: printed for the Brethren's Society for the Furtherance of the Gospel among the Heathen: and sold by J. Dodsley; T. Becket; W. Sandby; S. Bladon; E. and C. Dilly; and at all the Brethren's chapels, 1767.* 2v. (405, 497p.); plates (some folding); maps.

With illustrations of the indigenous people. The original German edition was published in 1765. IFP114

Croley, George. *See*: **Roberts, David**, *The Holy Land.*

Crouch, Nathaniel. The English hero: or, Sir Fran. Drake reviv'd. ... a full account of the ... acheivements of that ... renowned commander ... by R.B. The fifth edition. *London: printed for N. Crouch, 1698.* [4], 174, [14]p.; plate. Wing 7322aA.

A biographical description of Drake and his voyages, mainly to the West Indies and South America. 'R.B.' stands for Robert (or Richard) Burton, pseudonym of Crouch.

Copy lacks title-page. Previous owner: Lee Warly. IFP115

Cruttwell, Clement. The new universal gazetteer; or, geographical dictionary: containing a description of all the empires, kingdoms, states ... in the known world; with the government, customs, manners, and religion of the inhabitants ... with twenty-eight whole sheet maps. Second edition. *London: printed for Longman, Hurst, Rees, and Orme, and Cadell and Davies, 1808. 4v + atlas.*

Ideal for finding names of places mentioned in travel texts, which modern atlases may no longer show. IFP116

Cuba; or the policy of England, Mexico, and Spain, with regard to that island. By an Englishman. *London: James Ridgway, 1830. 22p.*

Concerns the Spanish-Mexican War, 1829–1830. IFP117

Cui Bono? Or, the prospects of a free trade in tea. A dialogue between an antimonopolist and a proprietor of East India stock. *London: J. Hatchard and Son, 1833. [4], 38p.*

Half-title dedication: 'From the Author'. IFP118

Cunningham, John William. Church of England missions. *London: printed for J. Hatchard, and sold by L.B. Seeley, 1814. [4], 43p.*

Discusses the state of the Church of England missions in the East and possible causes for and solutions to the 'absence of the missionary spirit in the Establishment'. IFP119

Cursetjee, Manockjee. The Chairman of the Select Committee of Parliament to inquire into the operation of Act 3 and 4 William IV, cap. 85, "For the better Government of Her Majesty's Indian Territories". *[Bombay?]: [1853]. 4p.*

A letter, dated Bombay 29 March 1853, on the renewal of the East India Company's Charter.

Title-page dedication: 'For Sir R H Inglis'. IFP120

D., S. A letter to S^r. John Eyles, ... Sub-Governour of the South-Sea Company, ... occasioned by the debates at the last General Court. The second edition, corrected. *London: printed for John Brotherton; and sold by A. Dodd, 1732. 7, [1]p.*

Letter signed 'S.D.' — Queries the extent of indebtedness of the Company. IFP121

Dalrymple, Alexander. Considerations on a pamphlet entitled "Thoughts on our acquisitions in the East-Indies, particularly respecting Bengal". *London: printed in the year 1772, and sold by J. Nourse; and P. Elmsly; Brotherton and Sewell; and J. Robson, 1772. 71, [1]p.*

In reply to George Johnston. IFP122

— A general view of the East-India Company, written in January 1769, to which are added some observations on the present state of their affairs. *London: printed 1772, and sold by J. Nourse and P. Elmsly; Brotherton and Sewell; J. Robson; and S. Leacroft, 1772. vii, [1], 109, [1]p.*

Includes a history of trade between European countries and the East. IFP123

— A plan for extending the commerce of this kingdom, and of the East-India-Company. *London: printed for the author; and sold by J. Nourse, and T. Payne, 1769. [4]. 111, [1]p.*

On opportunities for extending trade with Borneo and the Philippines. IFP124

— The rights of the East-India Company. *[London?]: [1773]. 20p.* IFP125

— *See also*: **I am also inclined to respect.**

Darwin, Charles. Journal of researches into the natural history and geology of the countries visited during the voyage of H.M.S. Beagle round the world, under the command of Capt. Fitz Roy. Second edition, corrected, with additions. *London: John Murray, 1845. 3 parts: viii, 519p. Murray's Home and Colonial Library, Nos. XII–XIV.*

Previous owner: 'Robert Harry Inglis'. IFP126

Davis, John. Travels of four years and a half in the United States of America ... 1798, 1799, 1800, 1801 and 1802. *London: sold by T. Ostell and T. Hurst; B. Dugdale, and J. Jones, Dublin; and H. Caritat, New-York; for R. Edwards, Bristol, 1803.* 454p.
The author travelled through southern America meeting both 'negroes' and 'gentlemen' and writing a 'commentary and account of human nature'. An interesting evolutionist account of early colonised America. IFP127

Dickinson, John. The government of India under a bureaucracy. *London: Saunders & Stanford; Simms & Dinham, Manchester, 1853.* vi, [2], 146, [2]p.
India Reform Tracts, no. VI. Describes the interaction between the British and native cultures of India, in areas such as justice and revenue. IFP128

A Digest of the despatches on China ... with a connecting narrative and comments. *London: James Ridgway, 1840.* [4], 240p.
Includes Captain Charles Elliot's narratives and opinions, Lord Palmerston's directions, reports of the Opium trade in 1837, and descriptions of events such as the 'execution of a native in front of the factories'.
Title-page dedication: 'From the Author'. IFP129

Discovery of the Islands of Salomon. *In*: Churchill's *Collection of voyages and travels,* London, 1732, vol. 4, pp.622–635.
Incomplete, lacks the beginning and end. Information is scarce on the Solomon Islands, discovered by the Spanish about 1695.

Dixon, Captain George. A voyage round the world; but more particularly to the north-west coast of America: ... 1785, 1786, 1787 and 1788 ... Dedicated, by kind permission to Sir Joseph Banks. The second edition. *London: Geo. Goulding, 1789.* xxix, [3], 360, 47, [1]p.; plates (some folding); maps; music.
With a crew that originally joined Cook's voyages, this expedition aimed to establish fur trade between the American coast and China. Includes details on the Sandwich (Hawaiian) Islanders. IFP130

Dobbs, Arthur. An account of the countries adjoining to Hudson's Bay, in the north-west part of America ... The whole intended to shew the great probability of a north-west passage, so long desired. *London: printed for J. Robinson, 1744.* [2], ii, 211, [1]p.; folding plate; map.
With an abstract of Captain Middleton's journey to the Orkneys and maps. IFP131

Documents explanatory of the case of Sir John MacPherson, Baronet, as Governor General of Bengal. *[London]: Printed by W. Bulmer and Co., [1800?].* vii, [1], 67p.
Title-page dedication: 'To Sir Hugh Inglis Bart'. Book-stamp of R.H. Inglis. IFP132

Du Halde, Jean Baptiste. The general history of China. Containing a ... description of the empire of China, Chinese-Tartary, Corea and Thibet. Including an extract and particular account of their customs, manners, ceremonies, religion, arts and sciences. Done from the French. *London: printed by and for John Watts, 1736.* 4v.; folding plates.
Du Halde's history is compiled from manuscripts and published journals and contains maps and plates. There are descriptions of each province, the emperors and nobility, some ceremonies and customs, the Chinese education system and scientific learning and recipes for healing, a history of the governments, and travels into Tartary and Korea.
Previous owner: Lee Warly (1746). IFP133

Dundas, Henry, *Viscount Melville.* Opinions of the late Lord Melville and Marquis Wellesley upon an open trade to India. *London: printed by E. Cox and Son, 1813.* [2], 18p.   IFP134

Duponceau, Peter. *See:* **Bromley, Walter,** *Appeal.*

Early travels in Palestine, comprising the narratives of Arculf, Willibald, Bernard, Sæwulf, Sigurd, Benjamin of Tudela, Sir John Maundeville, de La Brocquière, and Maundrell. Edited, with notes, by Thomas Wright. *London: Henry G. Bohn, 1848.* xxxi, 517p.
The texts range in date from the 8th to the end of the 17th centuries.
Presentation label in memory of Donald Robert Chalmers-Hunt, 1952.   IFP135

East India Company. Report of proceedings at a special General Court of Proprietors of the East India Company, held at the East India House, on Wednesday, 25th April, 1849. *[London?]: [1849].* 144p.
On the annexation of the territory of the Rajah of Sattara.   IFP136

The East India Question fairly stated. Comprising the views and opinions of some eminent and enlightened members of the present Board of Control. *London: James Ridgway, 1831.* iv, 52p.
Excerpts from writings of Robert Grant, Henry Ellis, and Charles Grant.   IFP137

Eastwick, William Joseph. Speech of Captain William Eastwick, on the case of the Ameers of Sinde, at a special court, held at the India House, ... 1844. *London: James Ridgway, 1844.* [2], 54p.
Special court of stockholders convened to protest at East India Company's actions.
Title-page dedication: 'Sir R H Inglis Bt MP'.   IFP138

The Edinburgh Reviewer refuted: being an exposure of gross misstatements in the leading article of No. CIV entitled 'The East-India Company – China Question'. *London: J. Hatchard and Son, 1831.* [6], 58p.
Signed 'Alethes' (p. 58). Second edition (half-title).   IFP139

Education in India. *[London]: G.N. Lemon, printer, Teddington, [1853].* 23p.
Previous owner: 'Robert Harry Inglis 15 July 1853'.   IFP140

Education in Persia and the East. *[London?], [1827?].* 8p.
About the missionary work of Joseph Wolff (see IFP513).   IFP141

Egede, Hans Povelsøn. A description of Greenland. Shewing the natural history ... the rise and progress of the old Norwegian colonies; the ancient & modern inhabitants; their genius & way of life ... with a new map of Greenland ... Translated from the Danish. *London: printed for C. Hitch; S. Austen; and J. Jackson, 1745.* xvi, [4], 220p.; folding plate; map.
With many maps and plates depicting people. Egede, a missionary, describes the beliefs and rites of the inhabitants.   IFP142

Egerton, *Lady* **Frances.** Journal of a tour in the Holy Land, in May and June, 1840. ... With lithographic views, from original drawings, by Lord Francis Egerton. *London: printed by Harrison and Co., 1841.* [8], 141p.; plates.
'For private circulation only; for the benefit of the Ladies' Hibernian Female School Society'.
Previous owners: Inscription of 'E.M. Bayley from her kind friend E.B. July 1841'. Book stamp of the Sailors' Home, Dover. Presentation label in memory of Donald Robert Chalmers-Hunt, 1952.   IFP143

Ellis, *Right Hon. Sir* **Henry.** Journal of the proceedings of the late embassy to China. *London: Printed for John Murray, 1817.* vii, [1], 526, [2]p.; 11 plates; folding maps.
The journal records a journey through Rio de Janeiro, Cape of Good Hope and Java on the way to China where the author meets the Emperor. Includes descriptions of processions, trade, laws, religion and expressions of belief.   IFP144

Ellis, Henry, *Governor of Georgia.* A voyage to Hudson's-Bay, by the Dobbs Galley and California, in the years 1746 and 1747, for discovering a north west passage; with an accurate survey of the coast, and a short natural history of the country. ... *London: printed for H. Whitridge, 1748.* xxviii, 336p.; plates (some folding); map.
Frontispiece: 'A new chart of the ... North West Passage'. Contains a history of previous attempts by Frobisher, Fenton and Weymouth.
Two copies.   IFP145

Ellis, William. Narrative of a tour through Hawaii, or, Owhyhee; with observation on the natural history of the Sandwich Islands, and remarks on the manners, ... history, and language of their inhabitants. Second edition, enlarged. *London: H. Fisher, Son, and P. Jackson. Hatchard and Son; Seeley and Son; Hamilton, Adams, and Co.; Sherwood and Co.; and Simkin and Marshall, London; Waugh and Innes, Edinburgh; and Keene, Dublin, 1827.* [8], 480p.; plates; map.
Frontispiece portrait of Ellis, 'Missionary from the Society and Sandwich Islands'.
Book label of W.H. Trimnell.   IFP146

Everard, Robert, *Seaman.* A relation of three years of sufferings of Robert Everard, upon the coast of Assada near Madagascar, in a voyage to India ... 1686. *In:* Churchill's *Collection of voyages and travels,* London, 1732, vol. 6, pp.257–282.
Tells of conditions of life for a seaman held captive by hostile 'negroes'. Includes information on seamanship, trading and warfare.

Faber, Ulrich. *See:* **Bry, Theodore de,** *America,* pts 7, 8.

Fabius. *See:* **A Letter to the Right Honorable the Earl of Buckinghamshire.**

Fellows, Charles. A journal written during an excursion in Asia Minor ... 1838. *London: John Murray, 1839.* x, [2], 347p.; ill.; plates.
Presentation label in memory of Donald Robert Chalmers-Hunt, 1952.   IFP147

Fenning, Daniel *and* **Collyer, Joseph.** A new system of geography: or, a general description of the world. Containing a particular and circumstantial account of all the countries, kingdoms, and states of Europe, Asia, Africa, and America ... *London: printed for J. Payne, and sold by J. Johnson, 1770[–1771].* 2v. (519, 788p.); plates (some folding); maps.
Book I: Asia; Book II: Africa; Book III: Europe; Book IV: America. Mainly geographical but includes much on the people of each area. With appendices on New Zealand, Oahena, Otahitee (Tahiti) and New Holland.   IFP148

Fernandes de Queiros, Pedro. *See:* **Bry, Johann Theodore de,** *India Orientalis,* pt 10.

Fernandez Navarrete, Domingo. An account of the Empire of China, historical, political, moral and religious. (1646–1673). *In:* Churchill's *Collection of voyages and travels,* London, 1732, vol. 1, pp.1–380.
Fernandez Navarrete was a Dominican Friar, who spent several years in China, learning the language, reading the histories and studying points of controversy among the missionaries. Observations are included on New Spain, the Philippines and parts of India. Translated from the Spanish.

A Few cursory remarks on Mr. Twining's letter... By a member of the British and Foreign Bible Society. *London: printed for J. Hatchard, by Stanhope & Tilling, 1807.* 15p.
Defends missionary activity against Twining's *Letter* (IFP484).
Two copies, one with the stamp of 'R.H. Inglis'.   IFP149

A Few observations upon the Report of the Select Committee of the House of Commons on New Zealand. *[London]: William Watts, [for the Aborigines Protection Society], [1844?].* 7p.
A criticism of the committee's views on the Maori and the Treaty of Waitangi.   IFP150

Fitzroy, Robert. Remarks on New Zealand, in February 1846. *London: W. and H. White, 1846.* 67p.
An account of the geography and recent history of New Zealand.
Two copies (one lacking pp.35–66, with a title-page with no date or imprint).   IFP151

Forbin, Claude de. Memoirs of the Count De Forbin, commodore in the Navy of France: ... containing his narrative of the voyages he made to the East-Indies, &c ... Translated from the French. The third edition. *London: printed for F. Noble, 1740.* 2v. (350, 306p.)
Forbin travelled to India, Thailand, Algiers, northern, eastern and south east Asia.
                                                                               IFP152

Fortis, Alberto. Travels into Dalmatia containing general observations on the natural history ... the arts, manners and customs of the inhabitants: in ... letters from Abbe Alberto Fortis. *London: printed for J. Robson, 1778.* [2], x, 584p.; plates (some folding); map.
Includes Fortis's edition of Archbishop Verancsic's *Iter Bude Hadrianopolim* in Latin. Gives details of funerals, costumes, and nuptial rites.   IFP153

Fox, Luke. North-west Fox, or, Fox from the North-west passage. Beginning with King Arthur, Malga, Octhur, the two Zenis of Iseland, Estotiland, and Dorgia; following with briefe abstracts of the voyages of Cabot, Frobisher, Davis, Waymouth, Knight, Hudson, Button, Gibbons, Baffin, Hawkridge: ... James Hall's three voyages to Groynland .... with the author his owne voyage, being the XVIth ... *London: printed by B. Alsop and Tho. Fawcet, 1635.* [10], 269, [3]p. STC 11221.   IFP154

Franklin, *Sir* John. Narrative of a journey to the shores of the Polar Sea, ... 1819, 20, 21, and 22. *London: John Murray, 1823.* xvi, 768p.; 35 plates; folding maps (some coloured).
Includes accounts of North American Indians and their involvement with western geographers. Additional contributions by J. Richardson, J. Sabine and R. Hood.   IFP155

— Narrative of a second expedition to the shores of the Polar Sea, in the years 1825, 1826, and 1827 ... including an account ... of a detachment to the eastward, by John Richardson. *London: John Murray, 1828.* xxiv, 320, clvii, [2]p.; 37 plates; maps (some folding, some coloured).
Includes meteorological and statistical information.   IFP156

Free trade with India. An enquiry into the true state of the question at issue between His Majesty's ministers, the honorable the East India Company, and the public at large ... By Common Sense. Second edition. *London: sold by Mesrs. Sherwood, Neely & Jones, 1813.* 22p.
MS note on title-page: 'With new preface'.   IFP157

Frezier, Amédée François. A voyage to the South-Sea, and along the coasts of Chili and Peru, in the years 1712, 1713 and 1714. ... With a postscript by Dr. Edmund Halley, ...

and an account of … the Jesuits in Paraguay. *London: printed for Jonah Bowyer, 1717.* [12], 335, [9]p.; plates (some folding); maps.

Sent to explore the South-Sea in competition with the Spaniards, Frezier records his impressions of the people, their music, clothes, myths and festivals.

Previous owners: Sophia Beck, Charlotte Beck.   IFP158

Friend of India, *see* **Shore, Frederick John.**

Fry, William Storrs. Facts and evidence relating to the opium trade with China. *London: Pelham Richardson; and sold by John Ollivier, 1840.* 64p.

Previous owner: 'Robert Harry Inglis'.   IFP159

Fryer, John. A new account of East-India and Persia, in eight letters. Being nine years travels, begun 1672. And finished 1681. Containing observations on … government, religion, laws, customs … of their housing, cloathing, manufactures, trades, commodities … *London: printed by R.R. for Ri. Chiswell, 1698.* [10], xiii, [1], 427, [1], xxivp.; plates (some folding); maps. Wing F2257.

Recording the natural history and geography of the places he visited, Fryer also provides insight into the people, noting their customs, material culture, dwellings, religion and rites such as burial. He visited Arabia, India and the Azores, focusing on Santiago (Cape Verde Islands) and 'Bombaim' (Bombay).   IFP160

Fuller, Andrew. An apology for the late Christian missions to India: comprising an address to the chairman of the East India Company, in answer to Mr. Twining; and Strictures on … a pamphlet, by Major Scott Waring. *London: sold by Burditt, and Button; also by Williams and Smith; printed by J.W. Morris, Dunstable, 1808.* [2], 93, [1], xxvi p.

Fuller was the Secretary to the Baptist Missionary Society. Discusses methods and morals of conversion in India, in answer to Twining (IFP484) and Scott Waring (IFP413 and IFP414).

Three copies: one has pp. 4–50 only, with a note on the first page 'The Title & Remainder of this Pam[phlet] will be published in a few days. 19th Jan.[ry] 1808.'   IFP161

— — Part the second. Containing remarks on Major Scott Waring's letter to the Rev. Mr. Owen; and on a "Vindication of the Hindoos, by a Bengal Officer." *London: sold by Burditt, and Button; also by Williams and Smith; printed by J.W. Morris, Dunstable, 1808.* 129, [3]p.

With a paste-on errata slip. In reply to Scott Waring (IFP417 and IFP418).   IFP162

— — Part the third. Containing strictures on Major Scott Waring's third pamphlet; on a letter to the President of the Board of Control; and on the propriety of confining missionary undertakings to the established church, in answer to Dr Barrow. *London: sold by Burditt, and Button; also by Williams and Smith; printed by J.W. Morris, Dunstable, 1808.* xii, 86, [2]p.

In answer to IFP255.   IFP163

Gale, Samuel, *Judge.* Notices on the claims of the Hudson's Bay Company: to which is added a copy of their Royal Charter. *London: John Murray, 1819.* 69, [2]p.

A condemnation of the North-West Company for the destruction of the Red River Settlement, published originally in Montreal in 1817 by Samuel Gale, judge of the Court of Queen's Bench at Montreal.   IFP164

Gatonbe, John. A voyage into the North-West Passage. Undertaken Anno. 1612. *In:* Churchill's *Collection of voyages and travels,* London, 1732, vol. 6, pp. 241–256.

Voyage undertaken by 'the Merchants Adventurers of London', Sir George Lancaster, Sir Thomas Smith, Mr Ball, Mr Cocken and Mr James Hall. With maps and diagrams.

Gellibrand, Henry. *See*: **James, Thomas,** *The strange and dangerous voyage.*

Gemelli-Careri, Giovanni Francesco. A voyage round the world ... in six parts, viz. I. of Turkey. II. of Persia. III. of India. IV. of China. V. of the Philippine-Islands. VI. of New-Spain. Written originally in Italian, translated into English. 1699(?). *In*: Churchill's *Collection of voyages and travels*, London, 1732, vol. 4, pp.1–572.

These full and accurate accounts include a rare description of the country inland of the American coast around 'Aquapulco' during a journey which began in 1693.

Ghose, Brij Kishore. The History of Pooree. *See*: **Strahan, James Morgan**, *Juggernauth.*

Gleig, *Rev.* **George Robert**. Sale's brigade in Afghanistan, with an account of the seizure and defence of Jellalabad. *London: John Murray, 1846*. Murray's Home and Colonial Library, No. XXXIV.

An account of the 13th Queen's Regiment and the 35th Bengal Native Infantry. IFP165

Gobat, Samuel. Journal of a three years' residence in Abyssinia, in furtherance of the objects of the Church Missionary Society. ... prefixed, a brief history of the Church of Abyssinia, by ... Professor Lee. *London: Hatchard & Son; and Seeley & Sons, 1834.* [2], xxi, 371, [17]p.; folding plate; map.

An account in the form of a diary. Includes a map and a history of Abyssinia. Deals with issues relating to missionaries' attempts to dispel superstitious beliefs and integrate with the local communities. IFP166

Gorges, *Sir* **Ferdinando**. America painted to the life. The true history of the Spaniards proceedings in the conquests of the Indians, and of their civil wars ... from Columbus ... to these later times. ... More especially, an absolute narrative of the North parts of America, and ... Virginia, New-England, and Berbadoes. *London: printed for Nath. Brook, 1659.* 4 pts; plates (1 folding); map. Wing G1302.

Previous owner: R.H. Inglis (stamp) IFP167

The Government system of education in India. *London: Seeley and Co., 1847*. 16p.

Reprinted from the *Calcutta Christian Observer*, February 1846. Attacks the system for being too secular. IFP168

Graham, Thomas, *Merchant of Bengal*. To the Honourable the Court of Directors for affairs of the Honourable United Company of Merchants of England, Traders to the East Indies. *[London?]: [1814?].* 62p.

Series of memorials by Graham protesting at not being appointed to the Supreme Council in Bengal. The same volume has a number of similar petitions addressed to the Court from Richard Sulivan (1784), John Lindsay (1812), and others. IFP169

Great Britain, Parliament. Petition presented to both Houses of Parliament; to the House of Lords by ... Lord Beaumont ... to the House of Commons by Joseph Hume ... *[London]: [1845].* 16p.

Opposes the deposition of the Rajah of Sattara. With a list of those signing the petition, and an analysis, by Rungo Bapojee, of the voting figures at the Court of the East India Company. IFP170

Great Britain, Parliament, House of Commons. Bury Hutchinson. *[London]: [1832].* 8p.

From the *Mirror of Parliament*, part cxlvii. On repayment of a loan by the late Bury Hutchinson to the Rajah of Travancore. IFP171

Great Britain, Parliament, House of Commons. The petition of the New Zealand Company, presented to the House of Commons by Joseph Somes, the governor of the company. *London: printed by Stewart and Murray, 1845.* 40p.
Signed by a number of other companies, banks, etc. Redress for previous actions is requested by the businesses involved.   IFP172

Great Britain, Parliament, House of Commons. Report from the Committee appointed to inquire into the state and condition of the countries adjoining to Hudson's Bay, and of the trade carried on there. *[London], 1749.* 60, xxxi, [1], 79, [1]p.
Includes a copy of the Company's Charter from Charles II, and the papers presented to the Committee.
Previous owners: bookplate of Sir Atwill Lake; inscription 'The property of Benjamin Harrison 1808'.   IFP173

Greaves, John, *Professor of Astronomy in the University of Oxford.* Pyramidographia: or a description of the pyramids in Aegypt; *[followed by]* A discourse of the Roman foot and denarius: from whence ... measures and weights used by the ancients, may be deduced. [1641]. *In*: Churchill's *Collection of voyages and travels*, London, 1732, vol. 2, pp. 625–674, 675–720.
Detailed description of pyramid and tomb-building, with line drawings.

Greaves, Joseph. *See*: **Jowett, William,** *Christian researches in Syria.*

Greenfield, William. A defence of the Surinam Negro-English version of the New Testament: ... a view of the situation, population, and history of Surinam, a philological analysis of the language, ... in reply to the animadversions of an anonymous writer in the Edinburgh Christian Instructor. *London: printed for Samuel Bagster, 1830.* iv, 76p.
Greenfield was superintendent of the editorial department of the British and Foreign Bible Society.   IFP175

Gregory, J. A manual of modern geography, containing a short, but comprehensive and entertaining account of all the known world; the situation, extent, product, government, religion, customs, &c. of every country ... This third edition is corrected and enlarged, ... A table of the latitudes and longitudes … By Emanuel Bowen. *London: printed for R. Hett; and Jer. Roe, Derby, 1748.* xii, 199, [11]p.
Includes details of the cultures and beliefs of each country. For example, 'the Mexicans have been called the most docile and civilized of all the Indians ... they take great delight also in dancing' (page 11).
Previous owner: Elham Parish Library.   IFP176

Grimshawe, Thomas Shuttleworth. An earnest appeal to British humanity, in behalf of Hindoo widows: in which the abolition of the barbarous rite of burning alive is proved to be both safe and practicable. Second edition. *London: Hatchard & Son, Seeley & Son; sold also by Westley; Nesbit; Blanchard; and all other stationers, 1825.* [2], 28p.
Has statistics on the incidence of immolation in the period 1815–1821.
Title-page dedication: 'Sir Rob. Harry Inglis from the Author'.   IFP177

Groser, William. What can be done to suppress the opium trade. *London: for the Committee of the Anti-Opium Society, by J. Haddon, sold by Pelham Richardson; J. Ollivier, 1840.* 29, [1]p.   IFP178

Groves, Anthony Norris. The present state of the Tinnevelley Mission. Second edition, enlarged. With an historical preface, and reply to Mr. Strachan's criticisms; and Mr.

Rhenius's letter to the Church Missionary Society. *London: James Nisbet and Co., 1836.* 36p.

Concerns Karl Gottlieb Ewald Rhenius's dismissal, in reply to J.M. Strachan (IFP461). Tinnevelley is modern Tirunelveli, near the Gulf of Mannar, southern India.　　IFP179

Guattini, Michel Angelo de *and* **Carli, Dionigi.** A curious and exact account of a voyage to Congo in the years 1666, and 1667. *In:* Churchill's *Collection of voyages and travels,* London, 1732, vol. 1, pp.553–589.

Written by two Capuchin monks whose account begins with a description of Brazil, prior to their sailing across to Africa and the Portuguese town of Loanda. Descriptions are given of the behaviour and manners of the people, their way of travelling, the produce of the country, and its rulers and religion.

Guillaume de Vaudoncourt, Frédéric. Memoirs on the Ionian Islands, considered in a commercial, political, and military, point of view; ... including the life and character of Ali Pacha, the present ruler of Greece. ... translated from the original inedited MS. by William Walton. *London: printed for Baldwin, Cradock, and Joy, 1816.* xv, [1], 502, [2]p.; plate; folding map.

Previous owner: J. Maitland, 32nd Regt.　　IFP180

Hakluyt, Richard. The principal navigations, voyages, traffiques, and discoveries of the English nation. 16v. *Edinburgh: E. and G. Goldsmid, 1884–90.* vols 1–3 only; plates.

Hakluyt was the first scholar to collect European navigations and voyages throughout the world, into one work (first edition published in 1599). Edited with an introduction by Edmund Goldsmid. Arranged by geographical area: Vol. I: Northern Europe, Vol. II: Eastern Europe and the Muscovy Company, and Vol. III: North-eastern Europe and adjacent countries.　　IFP181

Halkett, John. Historical notes respecting the Indians of North America: with remarks on the attempts made to convert and civilise them. *London: printed for Archibald Constable and Co. Edinburgh; and Hurst, Robinson, & Co., 1825.* vii, [1], 408p.

A description of the character, history and conversion of the 'natives', largely critical of European missionaries, with information on law and government.　　IFP182

— Statement respecting the Earl of Selkirk's settlement of Kildonan, upon the Red River in North America; its destruction in 1815 and 1816; and the massacre of Governor Semple and his party. *London: 1817.* [4], 125, [1], lxxxixp.; plate; folding map.

Preface dated January 1817. Attributed to John Halkett (British Library). With a map of Hudson's Bay territory, and Appendix of documents and depositions.

Previous owner: M.F. Smith.　　IFP183

— Statement respecting the Earl of Selkirk's settlement upon the Red River in North America; its destruction in 1815 and 1816; and the massacre of Governor Semple and his party. With observations upon a recent publication entitled "A narrative of occurrences in the Indian countries," &c. *London: John Murray, 1817.* viii, 194, c p.; plate; folding map.

Preface dated June 1817. 'A narrative' by Samuel Hull Wilcocke.　　IFP184

Hamel, Hendrik. An account of the shipwreck of a Dutch vessel on the coast of the Isle of Quelpaert, together with the description of the Kingdom of Corea. Translated out of French. *In:* Churchill's *Collection of voyages and travels,* London, 1732, vol. 4, pp.573–595.

By a Dutch seaman who escaped after thirteen years enforced residence in Korea, following a shipwreck in 1653. Quelpaert is modern Cheju Do, south of Korea.

Hancock, John. Observations on the climate, soil, and productions of British Guiana, and on the advantages of emigration to, and colonizing ... of, that country. Second edition. *London: published for the author, 1840.* [4], 92p.　　　　　　　　　　IFP186

Hanson, Richard Davies. Extracts from a letter to Captain Fitz-Roy. *[Not published]: 1846.* 16p.

Hanson, 'lately Commissioner of Requests in New Zealand', speaks out for the rights of the Maori people.

Previous owner: 'Robert Harry Inglis'.　　　　　　　　　　　　　　　IFP187

— Extracts from a letter to Governor Hobson. *[N.pl.]: 1842.* 8p.

Hanson, 'Crown prosecutor in New Zealand', discusses a land dispute between the New Zealand Company and a Maori chief.　　　　　　　　　　　　　　IFP188

Hanway, Jonas. An historical account of the British trade over the Caspian sea: with the author's journal of travels ... through Russia into Persia ... To which are added, The Revolutions of Persia ... with the ... history of ... Nadir Kouli. *London: printed for T. Osborne, D. Browne, T. and T. Longman, C. Davis, C. Hitch and L. Hawes, A. Millar, J. Whiston and B. White, R. Dodsley, and J. and J. Rivington, 1754.* 2v. (460, 460p.); plates (some folding); maps.

A personal journal giving details of cultural contact between different peoples. Part II, *Reflections*, describes Central Asia.

Previous owner: bookplate of Matthew Harrison.　　　　　　　　　　IFP189

Harding, E. The Costume of the Russian empire. *London: printed for E. Harding; R. H. Evans; J. White; R. Faulder; Dulau and Co.; J. Archer, Dublin; Bossange, Masson, and Besson, Paris; Perthez, Hamburgh; Lagarde, Berlin; Gay, Moscow; Fryber, Stockholm; La Motte, Petersburgh, 1803.* [c.150p.]; plates (coloured).

Colour plates of people and their costume, as seen through nineteenth-century eyes. With text naming other travellers' accounts.　　　　　　　　　　IFP190

Hardy, Robert Spence. The British government and the idolatry of Ceylon. *London: Crofts and Blenkarn; and sold by J. Mason, and J. Snow; also by H. Bellerby, York, 1841.* 58p.

Concerns Buddhism, temple donations and religious festivals.

Title-page dedication: 'Robert Harry Inglis from Revd Dr Bunting Jan. 6 1841'.　IFP191

Harmon, Daniel Williams. A journal of voyages and travels in the interiour of North America, between the 47th and 58th degree of north latitude, extending from Montreal nearly to the Pacific Ocean ... a concise description of ... the country, its inhabitants ... and the two languages, most extensively spoken. *Andover [Vermont]: printed by Flagg and Gould, 1820.* 432p.; [2] plates; folding map.

Information on trade, geography, languages and conversion, and material relating to the Indians as indigenous occupiers of this part of empire. An appendix: 'A general account of the Indians', with a vocabulary of the Cree and Tacully languages.　　　IFP192

Harriot, Thomas. *See:* **Bry, Theodore de,** *America,* pt 1.

Hawkesworth, John. An account of the voyages undertaken ... for making discoveries in the Southern hemisphere, and successively performed by Commodore Byron, Captain Wallis, Captain Carteret, and Captain Cook ... Drawn up from the journals ... of Joseph Banks. *London: printed for W. Strahan; and T. Cadell, 1773.* 3v. (139, 363–676; 410; 411–799p.); plates (many folding); maps.　　　　　　　　　　　　IFP193

Head, *Sir* **Francis Bond.** Rough notes taken during some rapid journeys across the pampas and among the Andes. Fourth edition. *London: John Murray, 1846.* ix, 160p. Murray's Home and Colonial Library, No. XXXVIII.   IFP194

Heber, Reginald, *Bp.* Narrative of a journey through the upper provinces of India, from Calcutta to Bombay, 1824–1825. (With notes upon Ceylon,) ... a journey to Madras and the southern provinces, 1826, and letters written in India. By ... Reginald Heber, ... Second edition. *London: John Murray, 1828.* 3v. (450, 564, 527p.), plate.

List of subscribers for amonument to Heber at end of vol 3.   IFP 195

Henchman, Thomas. Observations on the reports of the Directors of the East India Company, respecting the trade between India and Europe. *London: printed by T. Gillet, 1801.* iv, 229p.

With an appendix at the end containing the papers referred to in the work.   IFP196

Herbelot, Barthélemy d'. Bibliothèque orientale, ou dictionnaire universel contenant tout ce qui fait connoître les peuples de l'Orient ... leurs religions ... les arts et les sciences, ... les vies de leurs saints, ... *A La Haye: aux depens de J. Neaulme & N. van Daalen [colophon:] imprimé chez Jaques van Karnebeek, 1777 [–1779].* 4v.

Previous owner: bookplate of Abp William Howley.   IFP197

Herbert, *Sir* **Thomas.** Some years travels into divers parts of Africa, and Asia the Great. Describing more particularly the Empires of Persia and Industan ... severally relating their religion, language, customs and habit: as also proper observations concerning them. Fourth impression. *London: printed by R. Everingham, for R. Scot, T. Basset, J. Wright, and R. Clavell, 1677.* [6], 399, [19]p.; plates; maps. Wing H1536.

Rich anthropological material in the form of pictures and text. For example, on page 168, countries described include South Africa, Tenerife, Mauritius, India, Egypt and Iran.

Previous owner: Lee Warly (1755).   IFP198

Herrera Tordesillas, Antonio de. The general history of the vast continent and islands of America, commonly call'd the West-Indies, from the first discovery thereof ... collected from original relations sent to the Kings of Spain. *London: printed for Jer. Batley, 1725.* 6v.; folding plates; maps.

With a portrait of Christopher Columbus in volume one. Describes the understandings and misunderstandings between the visitors and visited.   IFP199

— *See also*: **Barbot, Jean,** *Description*; **Bry, Theodore de,** *America*, pt 12.

Hinds, Samuel. The latest official documents relating to New Zealand; with introductory observations. *London: John W. Parker, 1838.* 46, [1]p.

An appeal to take New Zealand under British crown protection. Documents include letters from Sir R. Bourke, Captain W. Hobson and James Busby.   IFP200

Hodges, William. Travels in India, during the years 1780, 1781, 1782, & 1783. *London: printed for the author, and sold by J. Edwards, 1793.* vi, 156, [2]p.

With many engravings of people, landscapes and antiquities, as well as copies of Indian paintings.   IFP201

Holloway, William. Notes on Madras judicial administration. *Madras: published for J. Higginbotham, by C.M. Pereyra, at the Price Current Press, 1853.* [2], 60, iv p.

A defence of the Madras judges, in reply to John Bruce Norton's *The administration of justice in Southern India* (IFP328).   IFP202

Holmes, W. D. Report on steam communication with India via the Red Sea. Fourth edition. *London: John Weale, 1838. Reprinted, 1840.* 52p.; folding plate; table.

Proposal for a precursor of the Suez Canal route, using omnibuses between Cairo and Suez. IFP203

Holwell, John Zephaniah. An address to the proprietors of East India Stock; setting forth the unavoidable necessity and real motives for the revolution in Bengal, in 1760. *London: printed for T. Becket and P.A. de Hondt, 1764.* 80p. IFP204

— Mr Holwell's refutation of a Letter from certain gentlemen of the Council at Bengal, to the Honourable the Secret Committee. Serving as a supplement to his Address to the proprieters of East-India stock. *London: printed for T. Becket and P. A. de Hondt, 1764.* 35, [1]p.

In response to Sir E. Coote's *Letter to the East India Company* (IFP111). IFP205

Hooker, Joseph Dalton. Elevation of the great table land of Thibet. *[London]: [1849].* 8p. Periodical offprint? Ed. with foreword by W. J. Hooker. Incomplete? IFP206

— Notes of a tour in the plains of India, the Himala, and Borneo; being extracts from the private letters of Dr. Hooker, written during a government botanical mission to those countries. *London: Reeve, Benham and Reve, 1848–1849.* 2 pts (41 [i.e. 59], 106p.).

Includes visits to Egypt and Malta. IFP207

Horsley, Samuel. *See*: **Vincent, William,** *The voyage of Nearchus.*

Howell, James. Instructions for forreine travell. *London: printed by T. B. for Humprey* [sic] *Mosley, 1642.* [10], 236p. Wing H3082.

Ideas and principles concerning contemporary travel.

Two copies; one with previous owners: Henry Oxinden of Barham; Lee Warly IFP208

Hübner, Johann, *the Elder.* A new and easy introduction to the study of geography, by way of question and answer. Principally designed for the use of schools: in two parts ... I. An explication of the sphere ... II. A general description of all the most remarkable countries throughout the world; of their respective situations ... customs, forms of government and religion &c. The third edition, carefully revised and corrected by J. Cowley, Geographer to his Majesty. *London: printed for T. Cox; and J. Hodges, 1746.* vi, 271, [23]p.; 29 maps; ill.

Translated from the German. Includes descriptions of the people: e.g. of the inhabitants of the Unknown Countries: 'According to the account the Dutch give of it, they are a people of small stature, having large heads, broad faces, and flat noses ... both men and women have no other business than that of hunting and fishing'.

Previous owner: Lee Warly (1746). IFP209

Hudson's Bay Company. An ordinance for the more effectual administration of justice, in the Colony of Rupertsland. *[London]: [Hudson's Bay Company], [1822?].* 80p.

The text has numbered paragraphs. IFP210

— [Ordinance]. The Governor of Rupert's Land, is Governor-in-Chief of all the territories of the Hudson's Bay Company, ... *[London], [1830?].* 79p.

No preamble; unnumbered paragraphs. IFP211

Huie, James A. History of Christian missions from the Reformation to the present time. *Edinburgh; London: Oliver & Boyd; and Simpkin, Marshall, 1842.* 346, [2]p.

The book charts the missions of the Catholic and Protestant churches to Eastern Asia, America, southern India, northern India, Ceylon, western India, China, Africa, Greenland, Labrador, West Indies, Guiana, and Polynesia. IFP212

Hunter, John Dunn. Reflections on the different states and conditions of society; with the outlines of a plan to ameliorate the circumstances of the Indians of North America. *London: printed by J.R. Lake, 1823.* 20p.

Title-page: 'Solely for the use of the members of the New England Company'. Author signs introduction. IFP213

Hunter, William. Travels through France, Turkey, and Hungary, to Vienna, in 1792. To which are added ... tours in Hungary, in 1799 and 1800. In ... letters to his sister. *London: printed for J. White, by T. Bensley, 1803.* 2v. (412, 486p.); [12] plates (1 folding, coloured).

Records customs such as battles, marriages and institutions in the Mediterranean, Anatolia and eastern Europe. IFP214

Hutchins, Thomas. A topographical description of Virginia, Pennsylvania, Maryland, and North Carolina, ... An appendix containing Mr Patrick Kennedy's journal up the Illinois River, and a correct list of the different nations and tribes of Indians, with the number of fighting men, &c. *London: printed for the Author, and sold by J. Almon, 1778.* [2], ii, 67, [1]p.; folding plates; maps.

Mostly geographical, but the appendix provides information on the first contact with North American Indians. IFP215

'I am always inclined to respect the institutions ...' *[London?]: [1772?].* 17, [1]p.

A treatise on the governing of the East India Company, including anecdotes relating to the impact of commerce on the indigenous people. Refers to G. Johnston's anonymous *Thoughts on our acquisitions in the East-Indies* (1771) on the need for reorganisation in East-Indian government.

MS note on title-page: 'by Alex. Dalrymple'. IFP216

Indian Official. *See*: **The Judicial system of British India.**

Indus. Bombay briberies. *See*: **Bombay briberies.**

Institution for the Encouragement of Native Schools in India. The first report of the Institution for the Encouragement of Native Schools in India: with a list of subscribers and benefactors. *London: Black, Kinsbury, Parbury and Allen, 1818.* 67, [1]p.

Originally printed at Serampore.

Previous owner: 'R.H. Inglis'. IFP217

Irby, Charles Leonard *and* **Mangles, James.** Travels in Egypt and Nubia, Syria, and the Holy Land. *London: John Murray, 1845.* viii, 150p.

An account of a four-year tour in the Near East (1816–1820) by two commanders in the Royal Navy, describing the antiquities and indigenous cultures encountered. IFP218

Irwin, Eyles. An enquiry into the feasibility of the supposed expedition of Buonaparté to the East. *London: printed for George Nicol, 1798.* 22p.

On the risk to British eastern possessions from Bonaparte's campaign in the Mediterranean. IFP219

— A series of adventures in the course of a voyage up the Red-Sea, on the coasts of Arabia and Egypt; and of a route through the desarts of Thebais, in the year 1777: with ... a voyage from Venice to Latichea; and of a route through the deserts of Arabia, ... in ... 1780 and 1781. In letters to a lady. The third edition. *London: printed for J. Dodsley, 1787.* 2v. (387, 401p.); plates (most folding); maps. IFP220

Isenberg, Karl Wilhelm. Journals of the Rev. Messrs. Isenberg and Krapf, missionaries of the Church Missionary Society, detailing their proceedings in the kingdom of Shoa, and journeys in other parts of Abyssinia, in the years 1839, 1840, 1841, and 1842. To which is prefixed a geographical memoir of Abyssinia and South-Eastern Africa, by James M'Queen. *London: Seeley, Burnside, and Seeley, 1843.* xxvii, [1], 95, [1], 529, [1]p.; [2] folding plates; maps.

Previous owner: 'Thoˢ. Brockman from Sir T.D. Acland London, S. Mark's Eve 1844.'

IFP221

Ives, Edward. A voyage from England to India, in the year MDCCLIV. And an historical narrative of the operations of the squadron and army in India, under the command of Vice-Admiral Watson and Colonel Clive, interspersed with some interesting passages relating to the manners, customs, &c. of several nations in Indostan. Also, a journey from Persia to England. *London: printed for Edward and Charles Dilly, 1773.* xii, 506p.; plates (some folding); maps.

The journey from Persia to England was in 1758 and 1759. Both accounts are illustrated, and there is a map of Mesopotamia. Descriptions of the contact with local peoples for example, a drawing of the death rites of the Indians, and a translation of an Arabian seal or talisman.

Title-page inscription: 'Library of the Church of Cant[erbury]'.

IFP222

Jackson, Randle, *Barrister.* Substance of the speech of Randle Jackson, Esq. delivered at a general court of proprietors of East India Stock on Tuesday May 5, 1812. Upon the subject of a prolongation ... of the Company's exclusive charter. *London: printed for J. Butterworth; Black, Parry and Co.; J.M. Richardson; and J. Hatchard, 1812.* 62p.

IFP223

James, Thomas, *Captain.* The strange and dangerous voyage of Captaine Thomas James, in his intended discouery of the Northwest Passage into the South Sea ... With an appendix concerning longitude, by Henry Gellibrand ... and an advice concerning the philosophy of these ... discoueryes, by W[illiam] W[atts]. *London: for Iohn Legatt by Iohn Partridge, 1633.* [8], 120, [24]p.; folding plate; map. STC 14444.

Previous owner: Thomas Knapp (1722). Imperfect copy, lacking titlepage.   IFP224

— Captain Thomas James's ... voyage in his intended discovery of the North-West Passage into the South Sea, in the years 1631 and 1632 ... and the rarities observed, both philosophical and mathematical ... to which are added a plat [*sic*] or card for the sailing in those seas. Also divers little tables of the author's, of the variation of the compass, &c. *In:* Churchill's *Collection of voyages and travels*, London, 1732, vol. 2, pp. 429–488.

Includes an 'Appendix concerning longitude' by Henry Gellibrand.

Jocelyn, Robert, *Viscount.* Speech of Viscount Jocelyn, M.P., in the House of Commons, on the case of the Ameers of Upper Scinde ... 1852 ... with an appendix. *London: Smith, Elder & Co., 1852.* 49p.   IFP225

John, Christopher Samuel. On Indian civilization, or, report of a successful experiment ... in fifteen Tamul, and five English native free-schools; with proposals for establishing a separate liberal native school society. *London: printed for F. C. and J. Rivington, by Law and Gilbert, 1813.* iv, 50p.   IFP226

Johnson, Charles, *Captain.* A general history of the pyrates, from their first rise and settlement in the island of Providence, to the present time. With the remarkable actions and adventures of the two female pyrates Mary Read and Anne Bonny; ... The Fourth edition. Volume 1. *London: printed for, and sold by T. Woodward, 1728.* '443' [i.e. 447]p.; plates (some folding); map.

Previous owner: 'Blackmore'.   IFP227

— The history of the pyrates, containing the lives of Captain Misson, Captain Bowen ... intermixed with a description of Magadoxa in Ethiopia; the natural hatred and cruelty of the inhabitants to all Whites ... Volume 2. *London: printed for and sold by T. Woodward, [1726].* 413p.; plates.
Includes plates and descriptions of 15 pirates.
Previous owner: 'Blackmore'. IFP228

Johnson, Edward. A history of New-England. From the English planting in the yeere 1628. untill the yeere 1652. Declaring the form of their government, ... their wars with the Indians ... the names of all their Governours, ... *London: printed for Nath: Brooke, 1654.* [4], 236, [4]p. Wing J771. IFP229

Jowett, William. Christian researches in Syria and the Holy Land in MDCCCXXIII. and MDCCCXXIV. In furtherance of the objects of the Church Missionary Society. With an appendix containing the journal of Mr Joseph Greaves, on a visit to the Regency of Tunis. *London: printed by R. Watts. Published, for the Society, by L. B. Seeley & Son, and J. Hatchard & Son, 1825.* viii, [8], 515p.; [3] plates; maps. IFP230

— Christian researches in the Mediterranean, from MDCCCXV. to MDCCCXX. In furtherance of the objects of the Church Missionary Society. ... With an appendix, containing the journal of the Rev. James Connor, chiefly in Syria and Palestine. Third edition. *London: printed by R. Watts. Published, for the Society, by L.B. Seeley and Son, and J. Hatchard and Son, 1824.* viii, [8], 454, [1]p.; [2] plates; maps.
Connor's journal, from 1819–20, includes material on the Coptic and Greek Orthodox churches. IFP231

Juan y Santacilla, Jorge *and* **Ulloa, Antonio de.** A voyage to South America. Describing ... the Spanish cities, towns, provinces, &c. ... with reflexions on ... religion and civil policy; ... customs, manners, dress, ... whether natives, spaniards, creoles, indians, mulattoes, or negroes.... Translated from the original Spanish. The second edition. *London: printed for L. Davis and C. Reymers, printers to the Royal Society, 1760.* 2v. (498, 410p.); folding plates; maps.
A Franco-Spanish expedition to take astronomical and geographical measurements.
IFP232

The Judicial system of British India considered with especial reference to the training of the Anglo-Indian judges. By an Indian official. *London: Pelham Richardson, 1852.* 68p.
IFP233

Kaempfer, Englebert. A history of Japan: giving an account of the antient and present state and government of that empire ... Together with a description of ... Siam. Written in High Dutch ... and translated ... by J.G. Scheuchzer, ... with the life of the author ... To which is added, ... a journal of a voyage to Japan ... in ... 1673. . *London: for the publisher and sold by Thomas Woodward, and Charles Davis. 1728.* 2v. (612, 75, 11p.); plates (many folding); maps.
Records Japanese myths, trade, beliefs, politics, and their contact with other nations.
Engraved title in Latin precedes title-page: 'Historia imperii Japonici'. IFP234

Kempthorne, Sampson The large landed missionaries in New Zealand. A letter to ... Earl Grey, ... with an examination of the minute of the special committee of the Church Missionary Society on February 22, 1847. *London: J. Hatchard and Son, 1847.* 11, [1], 77p; 11p.

The text of the minute with own title-page: 'Church Missionary Society. New Zealand land question.' Discussion of the missionaries' involvement in the land disputes between colonisers and indigenous Maori people. IFP235

Kindersley, Nathanial Edward. A letter to the Earl of Buckinghamshire ... on the propagation of Christianity in India. *London: printed for J. Hatchard, 1813.* 16p. IFP236

King, James. Transactions during the second expedition to the north, by the way of Kamtschatka; and on the return home, by the way of Canton, and the Cape of Good Hope. *In*: Cook's *A voyage to the Pacific Ocean,* vol. III, book VI.

King, Richard, *M.D.* Narrative of a journey to the shores of the Arctic Ocean, in 1833, 1834, and 1835; under the command of Capt. Back, R.N. ... *London: Richard Bentley, 1836.* 2v. (312, 321p.); plates.
King was 'surgeon and naturalist to the expedition', a government-funded voyage intended to assist Sir John Ross's expedition and to make further geographical studies. The text comments on the native Indians' characters, customs, crafts, agriculture, material culture and the fate of the 'noble and intelligent races of the north'. IFP237

Knolles, Richard. The generall historie of the Turkes, ... to the rising of the Othoman familie: with all the notable expeditions of the Christian princes against them. Together with the lives and conquests of the Othoman kings and emperours. The fift [*sic*] edition. *[London]: printed by Adam Islip, 1638.* [10], 1500, [20], 31, [33]p. STC 15055.
Previous owners: John Lee (1720); Lee Warly (1740). IFP238

Kolb, Peter. The present state of the Cape of Good-Hope: or, a particular account of the several nations of the Hottentots: their religion, government, laws, customs, ceremonies, ... A short account of the Dutch settlement at the Cape. Written originally in High German, by Peter Kolben, ... done into English from the original by Mr. Medley. *London: printed for W. Innys, 1731.* 2v. (365, 363p.); plates (some folding). IFP239

Krasheninnikov, Stepan Petrovich. The history of Kamtschatka, and the Kurilski Islands, with the countries adjacent. ... translated ... by James Grieve. *Glocester: printed by R. Raikes for T. Jefferys, London, 1764.* [8], 280, [8]p.; plates (some folding); maps.
IFP240

Laborde, Léon de. Journey through Arabia Petræa, to Mount Sinai, and the excavated city of Petra, the Edom of the prophecies. *London: John Murray, 1836.* xxviii, 331p.; plates; map.
Presentation label in memory of Donald Robert Chalmers-Hunt, 1952. IFP241

La Mottraye, Aubry de. Voyages du Sᵣ. A. de la Motraye, en Europe, Asie & Afrique. ... Avec des remarques instructives sur les moeurs, coutumes, opinions &c. des peuples et des païs ... *A La Haye: Chez T. Johnson & J. Van Duren, 1727.* 2v. (472, 496p.); plates (some folding); maps. IFP242

Lane, Edward William. *See*: **Poole, Sophia,** *The English woman in Egypt.*

Langdon, William B. "Ten thousand Chinese things." A descriptive catalogue of the Chinese Collection, now exhibiting at St. George's Place, Hyde Park Corner; with condensed accounts of the genius, government, history, ... of the people of the Celestial Empire. Ninety-sixth thousand. *London: printed for the proprietor, 1844.* 170, [2]p.; ill.
Includes musical instruments, jewellery and clothes.
With an admission ticket pasted in (price One Shilling). IFP243

Lansdell, Henry. Russian Central Asia including Kuldja, Bokhara, Khiva and Merv. *London: Sampson Low, Marston, Searle, and Rivington. 1885.* 2v. (684, 732p.); plates (some folding); maps.
Frontispiece photograph of 'The Author in Khokand armour with saddle cloth presented by the Emir of Bokhara.' An account of the author's missionary travels in Russia starting in 1874, written for general readers and 'men of science and specialists'.
Dedication label: '30 April 1887. Presented to the Library of Canterbury Cathedral By the Author, Henry Lansdell'. IFP244

— Through Siberia. *London: Sampson Low, Marston, Searle, and Rivington. 1882.* 2v. (391, 404p.); plates.
Frontispiece photograph of 'The author in fish skin costume of the Gilyaks'.
Dedication label: '30 April 1887. Presented to the Library of Canterbury Cathedral By the Author, Henry Lansdell'. IFP245

La Peyrère, Isaac de. An account of Iseland [1644]; An Account of Greenland [1646]. *In*: Churchill's *Collection of voyages and travels*, London, 1732, vol. 2, pp. 381–395, 397–427.
Both accounts addressed to François de la Mothe le Vayer. La Peyrère was Secretary to the French Embassy at Copenhagen.

Lardner, Dionysius. Steam communication with India by the Red Sea; advocated in a letter to … Viscount Melbourne, illustrated by plans of the route, and charts of the principal stations. *London: printed for Allen and Co.; and Hatchard and Son, 1837.* 123, [1]p.; [6] plates; maps.
With a table of times and fares. IFP246

Larkins, William An address to the proprietors of India Stock from William Larkins, Esq. Accountant-General in Bengal, from July, 1777, to March, 1793. *London: printed at the Minerva-Press, 1798.* [3], 6–15, [1]p. IFP247

La Rochefoucauld Liancourt, François Alexandre Frédéric de, *Duke*. Travels through the United States of North America, the country of the Iroquois, and Upper Canada, in the years 1795, 1796 and 1797; with an authentic account of Lower Canada. *London: printed for R. Phillips [by T. Davidson]; sold by T. Hurst and J. Wallis, and by Carpenter and Co., 1799.* 2v. (642, 686p.); folding plates; maps.
Starting in Philadelphia and travelling west and north towards Ontario, then south and east again to Oswego and Boston, this account describes trade, laws, history and changes in populations and settlements after American independence. With descriptions of the social customs of the Cherokees, Shawanees and Mingoes, and their relationship with European settlers. With tables concerning trade and produce. IFP248

La Rochette, M. de. *See*: **Vincent, William,** *The voyage of Nearchus.*

Larpent, *Sir* **George.** On protection to West-India sugar. *London: printed for J. M. Richardson, 1823.* 71p.
MS note on title-page 'by Mr Larpent'. IFP249

— — Second edition, corrected and enlarged, and containing an answer to a pamphlet, entitled "A reply," &c. &c. by Joseph Marryat. *London: printed for J. M. Richardson; and for J. Hatchard, 1823.* 159p.
On the controversy surrounding trade and duty on West and East Indian goods. IFP250

Late resident in Bengal. *See*: **Shore, John,** *Considerations.*

Layman in India, A. *See*: **Wylie, McLeod,** *The urgent claims of India.*

The Author in Khokand armour   Henry Lansdell, *Russian Central Asia,* 1885. IFP244
The Author in fish skin costume   Henry Lansdell, *Through Siberia,* 1882. IFP245

Legh, Thomas, *M.P.* Narrative of a journey in Egypt and the country beyond the Cataracts. Second edition. *London: John Murray, 1817.* viii, [2], 296, [1]p.; 12 plates; folding map.
Contains accounts of the 'natives' in Nubia and Egypt as well as antiquities.   IFP251

Le Moyne de Morgues, Jacques. *See*: **Bry, Theodore de,** *America*, pt 2.

Le Poivre, Pierre, *see* **Poivre, Pierre.**

Lepsius, Richard. Discoveries in Egypt, Ethiopia, and the peninsula of Sinai, in the years 1842–1845. ... Edited, with notes, by Kenneth R.H. Mackenzie. *London: Richard Bentley, 1852.* xvi, 455p.; [3] plates; folding maps (coloured).
Letters from the author describing antiquities and details of life of the Turks, Bedouin and Nubians.   IFP252

Lery, Jean de. *See*: **Bry, Theodore de,** *America*, pt 3.

A Letter to a friend in England, on the state and patronage of the Church in India. By a chaplain on the Bombay establishment. *London: John Murray, 1829.* 59, [1]p.
Occasioned by the resignation of the Bishop of Calcutta.   IFP253

A Letter to Lord Althorp, on the China trade. Occasioned by an article in the "Edinburgh Review," No. CIV. *London: James Ridgway, 1833.* [4], 46p.
In reply to an article by J.R. McCulloch.
Title-page dedication: 'From the Author'.   IFP254

A Letter to the President of the Board of Control, on the propagation of Christianity in India: ... added, hints to those concerned in sending missionaries thither. *London: printed for J. Hatchard, 1807.* 23p.
Against Thomas Twining (IFP484).
Two copies; one with title-page dedication 'From the Author'.   IFP255

A Letter to the Rev. John Owen, ... in reply to the "Brief Strictures on the Preface to Observations on the present state of the East India Company." *London: printed for J. Ridgway. W. Flint, printer, 1808.* [4], 118, [2]p.
In reply to Owen's *Letter to John Scott Waring* (IFP341).
Two copies.   IFP256

Letter to the Right Hon. Charles Grant, President of the Board of Control, on British connexion with idolatry in Southern India. By a Madras civilian. *London: printed by G. Taylor, 1833.* 80p.
Concerning revenue from the pilgrim tax, etc. A large appendix of documents.   IFP257

A Letter to the Right Honorable the Earl of Buckinghamshire ... on the subject of an open trade to India. *London: published by J.M. Richardson, 1813.* 82p.
First of two editions of a letter regarding trade to India and its influence on the economy, the natives and the spread of British culture to them. Signed 'Fabius'.
The copy is marked up with MS corrections and additions for the second edition. With a MS attribution to Peter Auber.   IFP258

—— Second edition. 91p.   IFP259

Letters from Madras. *See*: **Maitland, Julia Charlotte.**

Levasseur, Guillaume, *sieur de Beauplan.* A description of Ukraine, containing several provinces of the Kingdom of Poland, lying between the confines of Muscovy, and the borders of Transylvania. Together with their customs, manner of life, and how they manage their wars. *In*: Churchill's *Collection of voyages and travels*, London, 1732, vol. 1, pp. 515–551.

Levasseur lived in Ukraine for 17 years from about 1640, and was mathematician and engineer to the King of Poland. Provides very exact descriptions of the countries around the Black Sea, and the habits of the Crim Tartars and Cossacks.

Lewin, *Sir* **Gregory Allnutt.** The opium question, as between nation and nation. By a barrister at law. *London: James Bain, 1840.* [4], 52p.
On China and the Opium War.
MS note on title-page identifies author as 'Sir Gregory A. Lewin'. Previous owner: 'Robert Harry Inglis'. IFP260

Lewin, Malcolm. Papers relating to the rupture between the Suddr Court of Madras and the government of the Marquis of Tweeddale. *London: printed by T. Brettell, 1848.* 56p.
Lewin complains over his dismissal as second Judge and over the actions of the first Judge, Waters.
Previous owner: 'Robert H. Inglis 30 March 1853'. IFP261

Lewis, Matthew Gregory. Journal of a West India Proprietor, kept during a residence in the island of Jamaica. *London: John Murray, 1834.* [6], 408p.
Includes comments on the relationship between the plantation owners and their work force. IFP262

The life and travels of Alexander von Humboldt. *See:* **Stoddard, Richard Henry.**

Lillie, Adam. Canada: its growth and prospects. Two lectures, before the Mechanics' Institute, Toronto ... With an appendix, containing information bearing upon the resources and position of the united counties of Leeds and Grenville. *Brockville, [Ontario]: David Wylie, printer, 1852.* [4], 60p.; tables. IFP263

Lindsay, Hugh Hamilton. Letter to the Right Honourable Viscount Palmerston, on British relations with China. *London: Saunders and Otley, 1836.* [2], 19p. IFP264

Linschoten, Jan Huygen van. *See:* **Bry, Johann Theodore de,** *India Orientalis*, pts 2, 3, 4, 10.

Locke, John. An introductory discourse, containing, the whole history of navigation. *In:* Churchill's *Collection of voyages and travels*, London, 1732, vol. 1, pp.ix–xciv.
Includes an annotated catalogue of 'most books of travel' in Latin, Italian, French and English (omitting any included in the volumes of the *Collection*).

Lobo, Jeronymo. A short relation of the River Nile, of its sourse [*sic*] and current; ... and of other curiosities ... written by an eye-witnesse who lived many years in the chief kingdoms of the Abyssine Empire. *London: printed for John Martyn, Printer to the Royal Society, 1669* [8], 105, [1]p. Wing L2733.
Translated from an anonymous Portuguese manuscript by Sir Peter Wyche.
Previous owner: James Long. IFP265

Long, John, *Trader.* Voyages and travels of an Indian interpreter and trader, describing the manners and customs of the North American Indians; with an account of the posts ... on the River Saint Laurence, Lake Ontario, &c. ... added, a vocabulary of the Chippeway language. ... A list of words in the Iroquois, Mohegan, Shawanee, and Esquimaux tongues, and a table, shewing the analogy between the Algonkin and Chippeway languages. *London: Printed for the author; and sold by Robson; Debrett; T. and J. Egerton; White and Son; Sewell; Edwards; and Taylor; Fletcher, Oxford; and Bull, Bath, 1791.* [2], x, [2], 295, [1]p.; folding plate; map.
Bookplates of 'Smith', and Benjamin Harrison. Stamp of 'I C'. IFP266

Lopes, Duarte. *See:* **Bry, Johann Theodore de,** *India Orientalis*, pt 1.

Lord, Henry, *Chaplain to the English Factory at Surat*. A discovery of two forreigne sects in the East-Indies, viz. the sect of the Banians, the antient natives of India, and the sect of the Persees, the ancient inhabitants of Persia, together with the religion and manners of each sect. *In*: Churchill's *Collection of voyages and travels*, London, 1732, vol. 6, pp.299–342.

Lord was preacher to the Honourable Company of Merchants, and his undated account gives a view of religions in India.

Loskiel, Georg Heinrich. History of the mission of the United Brethren among the Indians in North America. In three parts. Translated from the German by Christian Ignatius La Trobe. *London: printed for the Brethren's Society for the Furtherance of the Gospel: sold at No. 10, Nevil's Court, Fetter Lane; and by John Stockdale, 1794.* xii, 159, [1], 234, 233, [23]p.; folding plate; map.

Detailed description of the Indians of North America, including their character, initiation rites, dress, language, superstitions and arithmetic, and a history of the Christian missions there.   IFP267

Lynch, Frederic Thaddeus. A letter addressed to the Rt. Hon. John Sullivan, ... member of the Board of Controul. Second edition. *London: printed for the author, 1808.* vii, [1], 88p.

Accusations against Sullivan by the author, especially relating to the case of Sir Thomas Picton, Governor of Trinidad, and the action for libel brought by Sullivan against Draper.   IFP268

M., J. The rights of Jagannáth. *Calcutta: printed by J. Thomas at the Baptist Mission Press, 1852.* 20p.

Signed 'J.M.' On the government contribution to the temple of Juggernaut at Puri.
                                                                         IFP269

Macaulay, Colin. Two letters addressed to the Right Honourable General Lord Harris by Major-General Macaulay. *London: printed by Ellerton and Henderson. Sold by J. Hatchard, 1816.* [8], 123p.

An attack on Major Hart, Commissary for Grain during the Mysore campaign.   IFP270

— A third letter. *London: printed by Ellerton and Henderson. Sold by J. Hatchard, 1816.* [4], 42p.   IFP271

— A fourth letter. *London: printed by Ellerton and Henderson. Sold by J. Hatchard, 1817.* [2], 24p.   IFP272

Macaulay, Kenneth. The colony of Sierra Leone vindicated from the misrepresentations of Mr. Macqueen of Glasgow. *London: printed by Ellerton and Henderson; for J. Hatchard and Son; and Lupton Relfe, 1827.* vi, [2], 127p.

A defence of the colony's high mortality rate alleged by pro-slavers.   IFP273

Macaulay, Thomas Babington, Baron. A speech of T.B. Macaulay, Esq. M.P. on the second reading of the East India Bill, in the House of Commons. 1833. *London: T.C. Hansard, 1833.* 52p.

Favours retention of the powers of the East India Company in spite of its constitutional anomalies. From Hansard's *Parliamentary Debates*, Vol XVIII, third series.

Title-page dedication: 'For R.H. Inglis from T.B. Macaulay'.   IFP274

Macaulay, Zachary. East and West sugar; or, a refutation of the claims of the West India colonists to a protecting duty on East India sugar. *London: printed for Lupton Relfe; and Hatchard and Son, 1823.* viii [i.e. vi], 128p.

On the controversy surrounding trade and duty on West and East Indian goods, including references to slavery.
Previous owner: book stamp of R.H. Inglis. IFP275

Macdonald, Archibald, *Factor of the Hudson's Bay Company.* Narrative respecting the destruction of the Earl of Selkirk's settlement upon the Red River, in the year 1815. *London: printed by J. Brettell, 1816.* 14p.
An eyewitness account of the conflict with the agents of the North-West Company.
IFP276

Macdonald, Duncan George Forbes. British Columbia and Vancouver's Island comprising ... their physical character, ... natural history, ... also an account of the manners and customs of the native Indians. *London: Longman, Green, Longman, Roberts, & Green, 1862.* xiii, [1], 524, [1]p.; plate; folding map.
With descriptions of gold-mining and trade. Includes a study of those living in British Columbia at the time: the native Indians, the Chinese, and the British. IFP277

Macdonnell, Eneas. Letter to the Right Hon. Charles Grant, President of the Board of Commissioners for the affairs of India. ... demonstrating the injustice, impolicy and danger of the coercive and arbitrary measures instituted by that Board against the Directors of the East India Company; ... *London: Ridgway and Sons, 1834.* [4], 112, 34p.
Concerning relations between the Company and the King of Oudh. IFP278

Mackenzie, *Sir* Alexander. Voyages from Montreal, on the River Lawrence, through the continent of North America, to the frozen and Pacific oceans; in ... 1789 and 1793. With a preliminary account of the ... fur trade. *London: printed for T. Cadell, Jun. and W. Davies; Cobbett and Morgan; and Creech, Edinburgh, by R. Noble, 1801.* [2], viii, cxxxii, 412, [2]p.; [4] plates (some folding); maps.
With colour maps and examples of Chepewan vocabulary. IFP279

Mackinnon, Charles. Substance of the speech of Charles Mackinnon, Esq. at the East India House, 16th April, 1833, on the China trade, as reported in the debates on the renewal of the Company's charter. *[London]: [1833].* 8p.
Concerns the tea trade. IFP280

Madox, John. Excursions in the Holy Land, Egypt, Nubia, and Syria &c. including a visit to the unfrequented district of the Haouran. *London: Richard Bentley, 1834.* 2v. (436, 403p.); [27] plates.
Observations on antiquities, natural history and contemporary life. With a frontispiece portrait of 'The Author in his Turkish costume.'
Dedication label: 'Bequeathed by Rev. T. Brockman, late vicar of Saint Mary, Sandwich.' IFP281

Maitland, Julia Charlotte. Letters from Madras, during the years 1836–1839. By a lady. *London: John Murray, 1846.* ix, 145p. Murray's Home and Colonial Library, No. XXXV. IFP282

Mangles, Ross Donnelly. Wrongs and claims of Indian commerce. From the Edinburgh Review, no. CXLVI. *Edinburgh: printed by Ballantyne and Hughes, 1841.* [2], 44p.
Title-page dedication: 'Robert Harry Inglis'. IFP283

Marsden, William. The history of Sumatra, containing an account of the government, laws, customs, and manners of the native inhabitants, with a description ... of that island. The second edition. *London: printed for the Author, and sold by Thomas Payne and*

Son; Benjamin White; James Robson; P. Elmsly; Leigh and Sotheby; and J. Sewell, 1784. xii, 373, [7]p.; folding plate; map.   IFP284

Marsh, Edward Garrard. Statement. *[London]: [1851].* [2], 20p.
Not published. On land claims by missionaries in New Zealand, particularly concerning Archdeacon Henry Williams and the Church Missionary Society (see IFP90–IFP94 and IFP98–IFP101).   IFP285

Martin, Robert Montgomery. The Hudson's Bay territories and Vancouver's Island, with an exposition of the chartered rights, conduct, and policy of the Hon'ble Hudson's Bay Corporation. *London: T. and W. Boone, 1849.* vii, [1], 175, [7]p.; plate; folding map.
Title-page dedication: 'With Mr Martin's Compts'.   IFP286

— Opium in China, extracted from China; political, commercial and social. *[London?]: [1847].* [8], 90p.
With a dedication to the Queen.
Flyleaf has a signed presentation to Sir Robert Inglis dated 12 February 1847.   IFP287

— Reports, minutes and despatches, on the British position and prospects in China. *[Not published]: [1846].* xii, 132p.; folding plate; tables.
Half-title: 'British position and prospects in China'. Marked 'Private'. Including official information on the Opium War of 1839–1842, the Nanking Treaty of 1842, and Hong Kong.   IFP288

— The past and present state of the tea trade of England, and of the continents of Europe and America; and a comparison between the consumption, price of, and revenue derived from, tea, coffee, sugar, wine, tobacco, spirits, &c. *London: Parbury, Allen, & Co., 1832.* xi, [1], 222, [1]p.; folding plate; folding tables.
History and study of the development and economic and social effects of the tea trade with China. Also includes other trades such as in sugar, metals, and tobacco.   IFP289

Matheson, *Sir* James. The present position and prospects of the British trade with China; together with an outline of some leading occurrences in its past history. *London: Smith, Elder and Co., 1836.* [8], 135, [6]p.
With tables for the volume of imports and exports through the port of Canton in 1834 and 1835.
Title-page dedication: 'To Sir Robt. H. Inglis Bart M.P. with the Author's Complimens' [*sic*].   IFP290

Maundrell, Henry. A journey from Aleppo to Jerusalem at Easter, A.D. 1697. The fifth edition, to which is added ... the author's journey to the ... Euphrates ... and ... Mesopotamia. *Oxford: printed at the Theater, 1732.* [12], 145, [7], 10p.; plates; map.
Maundrell was chaplain to the Factory at Aleppo.   IFP291

— — The seventh edition. *Oxford: printed at the Theatre,* 1749. [12], 171p.; plates; maps.
Previous owner: Lee Warly (1760).   IFP292

Mauritius. A short appeal, to the House of Commons, in answer to the charges brought against the inhabitants of Mauritius. *London: printed by W. Glindon, 1836.* 30p.
Answer to John Jeremie's *Recent events at Mauritius*. The charges refer to accusations of illegal slave trading and fraud.   IFP293

May, Charles, *Mate in the Ship Terra Nova.* An account of the wonderful preservation of the ship Terra Nova of London ... homeward-bound from Virginia. *In:* Churchill's *Collection of voyages and travels,* London, 1732, vol. 6, pp. 345–354.

Describes the voyage of a merchant ship from August 1688 to April 1689, carrying the Duchess of Albemarle with family, retinue and rich belongings.

McQueen, James. *See*: **Isenberg, Karl Wilhelm,** *Journals.*

Meares, John. Voyages made in the years 1788 and 1789, from China to the north west coast of America. ... prefixed, ... a voyage performed in 1786, from Bengal, in the ship Nootka; observations on the probable existence of a north west passage; and some account of the trade between the north west coast of America and China; and the latter country and Great Britain. *London: printed at the Logographic Press; and sold by J. Walter, 1790.* viii, [12], xcv, [1], 372, [108]p.; plates (some folding); maps.

The first journal describes the people Meares met, from Ounalaschka island, near Alaska, to the coasts of China and Russia. In the second part, he describes the coast of America, but includes the Sandwich Islands (Hawaii) and Southern Pacific.   IFP294

Melville, Herman. Narrative of a four months' residence among the natives of a valley of the Marquesas Islands; or, A peep at Polynesian life. *London: John Murray, 1846.* 2 pts: xvi, 285p.; map. Murray's Home and Colonial Library, Nos. XXX–XXXI.   IFP295

Melville, William Henry Leslie. Remarks on the war in Afghanistan. *London and Edinburgh: William Blackwood, and Sons, 1842.* 27, [1]p.

Melville, of the Bengal Civil Service, denounces the war against Afghanistan. Concerns East India Company.   IFP296

Member of the British and Foreign Bible Society. *See*: **A Few cursory remarks.**

Merin, Joannes Baptista. A journey of John Baptist Merin ... to the mines of Hungary; with an account of his observations made there, in relation to them, and subterraneous passages in general. *In*: Churchill's *Collection of voyages and travels*, London, 1732, vol. 4, pp. 762–67.

Written around 1650, this short account covers such areas as the ways of draining mines and controlling 'noxious vapours'.

Merolla, Girolamo. A voyage to Congo and several other countries chiefly in Southern-Africk ... in the year 1682. *In*: Churchill's *Collection of voyages and travels*, London, 1732, vol. 1, pp.591–686.

Merolla was a missionary who travelled along the southern coast of Africa from the Cape of Good Hope to Angola and the Congo. He describes the River Zaire, the proceedings of the missioners, the superstitions and customs of the inhabitants, and the state of their war with the Portuguese, which he believes to be encouraged by the English and Dutch. Descriptions are included of the animals, birds and plants of the Congo and 'many curious things not taken notice of by the former missionaries'.

Mexican Iron Works. Prospectus of the Mexican Iron Works. Committee of Management. *London: printed by J. Darling, [1827].* 2 sheets.

A prospectus for 2,000 £20 shares in an ironworks at Zimapan.   IFP297

Mexico. The following information respecting Mexico, is conveyed in a letter from a gentleman long resident in that Republic ... *London: E. Wilson, 1827.* 15p.

Signed 'W.' — Head title: 'Mexican finances and dividends'.   IFP298

Middleton, Thomas Fanshaw. A letter from the ... Bishop of Calcutta, addressed to the Reverend Anthony Hamilton, Secretary to the Society for the Propagation of the Gospel in Foreign Parts. *London: S. Brooke, 1819.* 15p.

Concerning the establishment of a missionary college in Calcutta.   IFP299

Mignan, Robert. Travels in Chaldaea, including a journey from Bussorah to Bagdad, Hillah, and Babylon, performed on foot in 1827. With observations on the sites ... of Babel, Seleucia, and Ctesiphon. *London: Henry Colburn and Richard Bentley, 1829.* xvi, 333, [1]p.; [8] plates; folding maps.

A mainly architectural account of western Asia. Mignan also records his experiences as an English Christian in the Arabic world. IFP300

Moll, Herman. A view of the coasts, countries and islands within the limits of the South-Sea-Company. ... From the river Arancoa to Terra del Fuego, and ... through the South Sea ... The whole collected from the best authors, as well as manuscripts as printed. *London: printed for J. Morphew, 1711.* [4], 220p.

Lacks the map. IFP301

Monck, John. *See*: **Munk, Jens**.

Money, Edward. A letter on the cultivation of cotton, the extension of internal communication, and other matters connected with India, addressed to Sir Harry Verney. *London: James Ridgway, 1852.* 42p. IFP302

Montagu, John, *Earl of Sandwich.* A voyage performed by the late Earl of Sandwich round the Mediterranean in the years 1738 and 1739. Written by himself ... prefixed, Memoirs of the noble author's life, by John Cooke. *London: printed for T. Cadell Jun. and W. Davies, 1799.* [4], xl, 539, [1]p.; plates (1 folding); map.

Includes Greece, Turkey and Egypt. Illustrated with architectural drawings, maps, and inscriptions. IFP303

Montanus, Arnoldus. Atlas Japannensis: being remarkable addresses by way of embassy from the East-India Company of the United Provinces, to the Emperor of Japan. Containing a description of their several territories, cities, temples, and fortresses; their religions, laws, and customs, their prodigious wealth and gorgeous habits; ... with the character of the ancient and modern Japanners. Collected out of their several writings and journals by Arnoldus Montanus. English'd ... by John Ogilby. *London: printed by Tho. Johnson for the author, 1670.* [4], 488p.; folding plates; map. Wing M2485.

Records the history of European contact with Japan, and comments on the meeting of the two cultures.

Previous owner: Lee Warly (1757). IFP304

Montgomery, *Sir* **James.** Substance of the speech of Sir James Montgomery, Bart. in the House of Commons, ... on bringing forward his motion relative to the petition of Mr. John Pritchard, of the Red River settlement. *London: printed by J. Brettell, 1819.* 53p.

An attack on the North-West Company's actions following the destruction of the Red River Settlement. For Pritchard's account, see IFP364. IFP305

Moravians. Periodical accounts relating to the missions of the Church of the United Brethren, established among the heathen.. *London: published by the Brethren's Society for the Furtherance of the Gospel, 1790 [–1889].* 34v. Vols 1–15 only.

Letters, extracts and reports from Moravian missionaries in India, Africa and America, providing anthropological evidence of the impact of Christianity and the ways other cultures adapted it.

Previous owner: book stamp of R.H. Inglis. IFP306

Morgan, William, *naval architect.* Letter to the chairman of the Honorable Court of the East India Company, on the proposed communication with India, by means of steam navigation. *London: printed by Charles Skipper and East, [1835].* 43p.

Primarily a reply to an *Edinburgh Review* article (by Thomas Love Peacock, acc. *Wellesley Index*), and in support of Sir Pulteney Malcolm.

Title-page dedication: 'With Sir Pulteney Malcolm's Compliments'. IFP307

Morier, James Justinian. A journey through Persia, Armenia and Asia Minor, to Constantinople, in the years 1808, 1809 ... *London: 1812.* 2v. in manuscript.

Morier was 'His Majesty's Secretary of Embassy to the Court of Persia'; the manuscript covers the meeting of cultures in the Court of Persia and was published by Longman in 1812. IFP308

— — [A collection of reviews on Morier's *Journey*.] [London]: [1812]. 6 parts.

From *The Eclectic Review*, February 1812; *Proceedings of the Catholic Committee*, January 1812; *Lit. Pan.*, January 1812. IFP309

Morse, Jedidiah. A report to the Secretary of War of the United States, on Indian affairs, comprising a narrative tour ... illustrated by a map of the United States; ornamented by a correct portrait of a Pawnee Indian. *New-Haven: published by Davis & Force, Washington DC; Cushing & Jewett, Baltimore; W.W. Woodward, and E. Littell, Philadelphia; Spalding & Howe, and R.N. Henry, New-York; E. & E. Hosford, Albany; Howe & Spalding, Hartford; Richardson & Lord, S.T. Armstrong, Lincoln & Edmunds, Cummings & Hilliard, and G. Clark, Boston, 1822.* 96, 400p.; 2 plates; tables.

Morse, the Minister for the First Congregational Church in Charlestown near Boston, undertook a tour 'for the purpose of ascertaining, for the use of the government, the actual state of the indian tribes in our country'. It includes descriptions and histories of different tribes and their social customs, as well as discussion of the role they and their cultures have amongst the 'civilised' European colonies. Frontispiece portrait of 'A Pawnee brave, son of Old Knife'. IFP310

Morton, Nathaniel. New Englands memoriall: or a brief relation of the most memorable and remarkable passages of the providence of God, manifested to the planters of New-England in America; with special reference to the first colony thereof called New Plimouth ... *Cambridge [Mass.]: printed by S.G. and M.J. for John Usher of Boston, 1669.* [12], 198, [10]p. Wing M2827.

Blank leaf with the signatures of Johanna Eve, Elizabeth Eve, Richard Robinson (1733), Mary Tarington. IFP311

Mueller, Gerhard Friedrich. Voyages from Asia to America, for completing the discoveries of the North West coast of America. ... prefixed, a summary of the voyages made by the Rus[s]ians on the Frozen Sea, in search of a north east passage. Translated from the High Dutch ... by Thomas Jefferys. The second edition. *London: printed for T. Jefferys, 1764.* viii, 120p.; folding plates; maps. IFP312

Muhammad Ali Khan, *Nawab of Arcot.* Letter from Mahommed Ali Chan, Nabob of Arcot, to the Court of Directors. To which is annexed a state of facts relative to Tanjore. *London: printed for T. Cadell, 1777.* iv, 72p.

Concerns Tuláji, Rajah of Tanjore.

3 copies. IFP313

— Original papers relative to Tanjore: containing all the letters ... and the conferences which were held between his highness the Nabob of Arcot and Lord Pigot, on the subject of the restoration of Tanjore ... with ... Lord Pigot's last dispatch to the East India Company. *London: T. Cadell, 1777.* xix, [1], 134p.

Concerns the restoration of Tanjore to the Rajah Tuláji.

Three copies. IFP314

— Original papers, transmitted by the Nabob of Arcot to his agent in Great Britain: comprehending the transactions on the coast, down to the 10th of October, 1776. *London: printed for T. Cadell, 1777.* [4], 124p.
Concerns the restoration of Tanjore to the Rajah Tuláji.   IFP315

Munk, Jens. An Account of a … voyage perform'd by Captain John Monck in the years 1619, and 1620 … to discover a passage on that side, betwixt Greenland and America to the West-Indies … Translated from the High-Dutch original, printed at Frankford upon the Maine, 1650. *In:* Churchill's *Collection of voyages and travels*, London, 1732, vol. 1, pp.487–551.
Munk was described by the Churchills as 'one of the ablest seamen of his time'. Includes maps of Greenland and pictures of whales and whaling.

Murray, Alexander. Account of the life and writings of James Bruce of Kinnaird, Esquire, F.R.S. author of Travels to discover the Nile, in the years 1768, … 1773. *Edinburgh: printed by George Ramsey and Company, for Archibald Constable and Company, and Manners and Miller, Edinburgh; and Longman, Hurst, Rees, and Orme, London, 1808.* xiii, [1], 504p.; 22 plates; folding maps.
With appendices of Bruce's letters and minor writings. See IFP64.   IFP316

Mushet, David. The war with China: reflections on its source, progress, and probable event. *London: J. Hatchard and Son, 1840.* Lacks all after p.48.
A critical article, attacking British policy before the Opium War 1839–1842.   IFP317

N., W. Borneo. Remarks on a recent 'naval execution'. By W.N. *London: Effingham Wilson, 1850.* 47p.; plate. Additional leaf dated 17th January 1850 facing p.[35].
An account of Sir James Brooke's massacre of the Serebas and Sakarran in Borneo in 1849. The same pamphlet volume has other texts concerning the massacre, including Brooke's prosecution.   IFP318

Narayana, *Bhai*. Two Hindus on English education &c. Being prize essays by Náráyan Bhai and Bháskar Dámodar. *[Bombay], Printed at the Bombay Gazette Office, 1852.* viii, 71p.
Title-page dedication: 'With Sir Erskine Perry's Comp[liments]' (Perry was the President of the Board of Education, Bombay).   IFP319

New Zealand Company. The twelfth report of the directors of the New Zealand Company, presented to an adjourned special Court of Proprietors, on the 29th May, 1845. *London: printed by Palmer and Clayton, 1844.* 38p.   IFP320

— The eighteenth report of the directors of the New Zealand Company, presented to the annual general Court of Proprietors, on the 26th April, 1844. *London: printed by Stewart and Murray, 1845.* 120p.
Two copies.   IFP321

The New Zealand Company: its claim to compensation considered. *London: Seeley, Burnside and Seeley; Richardson; and Dalton, 1845.* 71, [1]p.
Concerns disputes over Maori lands.   IFP322

Nicolay, Nicolas de. Les navigations peregrinations et voyages, faicts en la Turquie … *En Anuers: par Guillaume Silvius, 1576.* [24], '308' [i.e. 210 leaves], [26]p.; ill.
Descriptions, with plates, of people in the Mediterranean, from Algiers and Italy to the Aegean islands and Constantinople,.   IFP323

Niebuhr, Carsten. Travels through Arabia, and other countries in the East, performed by M. Niebuhr, … Translated into English by Robert Heron. *Edinburgh: printed for R.*

Morison and Son, Perth; G. Mudie, Edinburgh; and T. Vernor, London, 1792. 2v. (454, 439p.); plates (some folding); maps.

With notes by the translator. The travels include Egypt, Sinai and the Yemen.　　IFP324

Nieuhof, Jan. Voyages and Travels, into Brasil, and the East-Indies: Containing an exact description of ... their provinces, cities, living creatures, and products; the manners, customs, habits, and religion of the inhabitants: with a most particular account of ... the revolt of the Portugueses, and the intestine war ... from 1640. to 1649. ... Translated from the Dutch original. *London: Awnsham & John Churchill, 1703.* [6], 369, [1]p.; plates (some folding); maps.

Nieuhof travelled with the West India Company to the Pacific Islands, including the Moluccas, 'Sumatera', 'Jakata', 'Amboina', and Taiwan, returning via the Southern Chinese coast, Malabar or Southern India, and the Persian Gulf back to his homeland in Holland.　　IFP325

— Voyages and travels into Brasil and the East-Indies. *In*: Churchill's *Collection of voyages and travels*, London, 1732, vol. 2, pp.1–326.

Divided into three parts: Brazil, 1640 (includes descriptions of the towns of Recife and Olinda; natural history; the inhabitants and the war between the Dutch and Portuguese); the East-Indies, 1653 (with maps and 82 woodcut illustrations of the islands of St Anthony and St Vincent, the Cape of Good Hope, China, and the coast of India and Persia, with particular attention to Batavia); the third section on East Africa (1672) was cut short by death of Nieuhof, presumed killed by natives in Madagascar.

Nimmuk. A letter to Sir James Weir Hogg ... on the salt monopoly of the East India Company, by Nimmuk. *London: James Madden, 1846.* 8p.　　IFP326

The Noozeed affair. A word for the people of India. Second edition. *London: Hatchard & Son, 1832.* 46p.

Concerns James Hodges, a member of the Council of Masulipatam, the East India Company, the Madras Presidency, Masulipatam District, Nozid zemindary. Appendices include a petition against an Act to discharge Hodges's loan.　　IFP327

Norton, John Bruce. The administration of justice in Southern India. *Madras: printed by Pharaoh & Co.; London: sold by V. & R. Stevens and G.S. Norton, 1853.* [2], 150, xlviiip.

Previous owner: 'Robert Harry Inglis 17 March 1853'.　　IFP328

— A letter to Charles Robert Baynes, Esq., ... containing a reply to his "Plea." *Madras: printed by Messrs. Pharaoh and Co., 1853.* [[2], 50p.

A reply to Baynes's defence of the Madras judges (IFP28) against Norton's charges of incompetence (IFP328).　　IFP329

Norwood, Colonel. A voyage to Virginia. *In*: Churchill's *Collection of voyages and travels*, London, 1732, vol. 6, pp. 145–170.

The voyage began in September 1649. Norwood finally landed in Virginia, but his party was abandoned and reduced to cannibalism in an attempt to survive. Found by Indians, Norwood and his party were given audience with the king who helped to arrange a rescue by representatives of the Governor of Virginia.

Notices on the claims of the Hudson's Bay Company: to which is added a copy of their charter. *London: John Murray, 1819.* 69p.

A defence of the Hudson's Bay Company concerning the destruction of the Red River settlement, placing the responsibility on the North-West Company.　　IFP330

Nouveau journal Asiatique ou recueil de mémoires, d'extraits et de notices relatifs à l'histoire, à la philosophie, aux langues et à la littérature des peuples orientaux. ... publié par la Société Asiatique. *Paris: Dondey-Dupré Père et Fils; Société Asiatique, 1822.* 1st series in 16 vols, 2nd series in 12 vols, 3rd series in 14 vols, 4th series in 6 vols. Maps. This journal covers all aspects of Asia, with maps, charts and references to language. Previous owner: bookplate of Charles Forster, B.D.   IFP331

Nowrozjee Furdoonjee. On the civil administration of the Bombay Presidency. By Nowrozjee Furdoonjee ... Published in England at the request of the Bombay Association. *London: John Chapman, 1853.* vii, [1], 88p.   IFP332

Nuremberg Chronicle. *See*: **Schedel, Hartmann.**

Observations on the report of the committee appointed to report the causes of the delay, in the trial of Warren Hastings, Esq. *London: printed for J. Debrett, 1794.* [4], 55, [1]p.   IFP333

Observations upon the Outline of a plan of emigration to Upper Canada. *London: printed by F. Warr, [1822?].* 8p.
A follow-up to IFP337.   IFP334

Oldmixon, John. The British Empire in America, containing the history of ...all the British colonies, on the continent and islands of America. *London: Printed for John Nicholson, Benjamin Tooke, and Richard Parker and Ralph Smith, 1708.* 2v. (412, 382p.); folding plates; maps; folding map as frontispiece to vol. 1.
Anonymous: dedication signed J. Oldmixon. Maps by Herman Moll. Covers both North America and the Caribbean.   IFP335

Oliver, James. Correspondence between Colonel James Oliver, and ... the Court of Directors for the affairs of ... the East India Company: with documents. *London: printed by G. Hayden, 1809.* [2], ii, 61, [2]p.
Concerning Oliver's dismissal by the Company. With two tables of financial figures for the administration of the Moluccas and Ternate in 1800–1803.   IFP336

The Opium question. *See*: **Lewin,** *Sir* **Gregory Allnutt.**

Outline of a plan of emigration to Upper Canada. *London: printed by F. Warr, [1822?].* 10, xv p.
Contains detailed costings of the expenses of transportation and settling. Appendix II by the founder of the Talbot settlement.   IFP337

Outram, *Sir* **James.** Baroda intrigues and Bombay khutput; being an exposition of the fallacies, erroneous statements, and partial quotations, recently promulgated by Mr. Lestock Robert Reid; in a "Letter to the editor of the Daily News." *London: printed (for private circulation,) by Smith, Elder, & Co., 1853.* vii, [1], 178p.
Concerns corruption and Colonel Outram's dismissal by the East India Company, in answer to IFP375.   IFP338

Ovalle, Alonso de. An historical relation of the Kingdom of Chile. By Alonso de Ovalle, of the Company of Jesus, a native of St. Jago of Chile and procurator at Rome for that place. Translated out of Spanish. 1649. *In*: Churchill's *Collection of voyages and travels,* London, 1732, vol. 3, pp. 1–138.
Describes the natural state of the country, its climate, wildlife, vegetation and inhabitants. Includes observations on the Spanish conquest, resistance to it, and attempts at peacemaking by Father Lewis de Valdivia. The final part discusses the propagation of Christianity among the native Indians.

Owen, John, *Rector of Paglesham.* An address to the chairman of the East India Company, occasioned by Mr. Twining's letter ... on the danger of interfering in the religious opinions of the natives of India, and on the views of the British and Foreign Bible Society, as directed to India. *London: printed for J. Hatchard; Black and Parry; and Rivingtons, by Stanhope and Tilling, Chelsea, 1807.* [2], 27p.

In reply to IFP484. IFP339

— — The third edition; ... containing Brief strictures on the "Preface" to Observation on the present state of the East India Company. *London: printed for J. Hatchard; Black, Parry, and Kingsbury; and Rivingtons. By Stanhope and Tilling, Chelsea, 1807.* [4], 36p.

In reply to IFP414.

Title-page dedication: 'With the author's best respec[ts]'. IFP340

— A letter to John Scott Waring, Esq. in refutation of his "Observations on the present state of the East-India Company ..." with strictures on his illiberal and unjust conduct towards the missionaries in India. *London: printed by Ellerton and Byworth, for J. Hatchard; J. Richardson; Black & Co., 1808.* [4], 82p.

By John Owen, acc. Halkett and Laing. In reply to IFP413 and IFP414.

Two copies. IFP341

Pagès, Pierre Marie François de. Travels round the world, in the years 1767, 1768, 1769, 1770, 1771. ... Translated from the French. The second edition, corrected and enlarged. *London: printed for John Murray, 1793* (vol.3: *1792*). 3v.; folding plate.

Volume I: America, the South Sea, South-east Asia and Java; Volume II: India and central Asia, Persia and Arabia; Volume III: South Africa, inland Africa, Siberia and the North and South Poles. IFP342

Park, Mungo. Travels in the interior districts of Africa: performed under the direction and patronage of the African Association, in the years 1795, 1796, and 1797. ... With an appendix containing Geographical illustrations of Africa. By Major Rennell. *London: printed by W. Bulmer and Co. for the author; and sold by G. and W. Nicol, 1799.* xxviii, 372, xciip.; plates (some folding); maps. IFP343

Parker, Samuel. Journal of an exploring tour beyond the Rocky Mountains, under the A.B.C.F.M. performed in the years 1835, '36, and '37; With a map of Oregon Territory. *Ithaca, N.Y.: published by the author. Mack, Andrus, & Woodruff, printers, 1838.* 371p.; [2] plates (1 folding); map.

Undertaken for the American Board of Commissioners for Foreign Missions. Describes the rituals, ceremonies, and daily lives of the Indians, including the Navaho and Fox. Also visits the Sandwich Islands (Hawaii) and describes the 'heathens', their temples and ceremonies and the impact of Christianity. IFP344

Parry, *Sir* **William Edward.** Journal of a second voyage for the discovery of a North-West Passage, from the Atlantic to the Pacific; performed in the years 1821–22–23. *London: John Murray, publisher to the Admiralty, and Board of Longitude, 1825.* [8], xxx, [2], 571, [1]p.; 39 plates; maps (some folding). IFP345

Paterson, William, *Lieutenant.* A narrative of four journeys into the country of the Hottentots, and Caffraria, in the years 1777, 1778, 1779. The second edition, corrected. *London: printed for J. Johnson, 1790.* xii, 175, [1]p.; plates (1 folding); map.

Records information on the dress, manners, appearance, living conditions and attitudes of the 'savage' people encountered in Africa. Includes an extract from Dr. Sparrman on the Hottentots. Other peoples included are 'Boschmans' and 'Caffres'. IFP346

Peck, Nathaniel *and* **Price, Thomas S.** Report of Messrs. Peck and Price, ... appointed at a meeting of the free colored people of Baltimore, ... delegates to visit British Guiana, and ... Trinidad; for ... ascertaining the advantages to be derived by colored people migrating to those places. *Baltimore: printed by Woods and Crane, 1840. London: reprinted by C. Richards, [1840].* 25p.   IFP347

Peggs, James. The government grant, to Juggernaut's temple: a letter to Henry St. George Tucker, Esq., Chairman of the Court of Directors of the ... East India Company. *London: Ward and Co., 1848.* 51p.   IFP348

— Voice from Ceylon. The present state of British connexion with idolatry in the island of Ceylon: a letter to ... Lord Stanley, Secretary for the Colonies. *London: published for the author, by John Snow, 1843.* 40p.; plate.
Frontispiece depicting 'A priest of Kandy, Ceylon'.
Title-page dedication: 'Sir R. Inglis M.P. From the Author Ilkeston June 1845'.   IFP349

— A voice from India. The present state of British connection with idolatry and Mahomedanism, particularly the government grant to the Temple of Juggernaut, ... A letter to ... Sir J.C. Hobhouse, ... President of the India Board. *London: John Snow, 1847.* 71p.   IFP350

Pellham, Edward. God's power and providence, shewed in the miraculous preservation and deliverance of eight English-men, left by mischance in Greenland ... 1630 ... with a description of the chief places and rarities of that barren and cold country. *In:* Churchill's *Collection of voyages and travels*, London, 1732, vol. 4, pp. 750–762.
Written by the gunner's mate of a Greenland fisher.

Perry, Thomas Erskine. On the geographical distribution of the principal languages of India, and the feasibility of introducing English as a lingua franca. *[Bombay?]: 1853.* [2], 29p.; folding map.
From the *Journal* of the Bombay Branch of the Royal Asiatic Society, January 1853. With a colour map of the linguistic regions in India. Head-title: 'The languages of India, and the function of English as a lingua franca'.   IFP351

Persico, *Rev.* **Ignatius.** *See:* **Strickland, William,** *Notes.*

Philip, Robert. Peace with China! or, the crisis of Christianity in Central Asia: a letter to ... T.B. Macaulay, Secretary at War. *London: John Snow, 1840.* 15, [1]p.
On the Opium war of 1839–1842.
Title-page dedication: 'With the Author's respects'. Title-page verso is folded as an envelope addressed to 'Sir R H Inglis Bart, 7 Bedford Square' and is stamped and franked with two penny stamps.   IFP352

Phillips, Thomas, *Captain.* A journal of a voyage ... 1693, 1694, from England, to Cape Monseradoe, in Africa; and thence along the coast of Guiney to Whidaw ... and ... to Barbadoes. With ... account of the country, the people, their manners, forts, trade, &c. *In:* Churchill's *Collection of voyages and travels*, London, 1732, vol. 6, pp.171–239.
Includes full details of the voyage, including plans and navigational tables. Descriptions of life in 'Guiney' (Guinea) and 'Whidaw' (Ouidah or Benin) include information on trade. Costs of various goods are given, and an analysis of the value of slaves (around three pounds fifteen shillings a head – the preferred payment being in cowries).

Pickering, John. Remarks on the Indian languages of North America. From the *Encyclopedia Americana*, vol. VI, 1831. *[Philadelphia]: Reprinted 1836.* [4]p., pp.[581]–600.

A comparative grammar of the Cherokee, Delaware and related languages.　　IFP353

Pigafetta, Filippo. *See*: **Bry, Johann Theodore de,** *India Orientalis*, pt 1.

Pinkerton, John. A general collection of the best and most interesting voyages and travels in all parts of the world. *London: printed for Longman, Hurst, Rees, and Orme; and Cadell and Davies, 1808–1814.* 17v.

Reproduces extracts and whole accounts from many sources, such as Hakluyt and the *Histoire Générale des Voyages,* and includes his own compositions based on first-hand sources.

Vol. I. Europe and beyond: Russia and Siberia; China; the North East Passage, Lapland, the North Pole; Spitzbergen, Iceland, the Azores.

Vols II–VI. Europe.

Vol. VII. Asia: China, East Indies, Tartary, India, Russia, Korea, Tibet, Japan.

Vol. VIII. Asia: India, East Indies.

Vol. IX. Asia: Persia, Tartary, Russia, Bakhara, Siam, Tonquin, Cochin China.

Vol. X. Asia: Arabia, Levant, Mesopotamia, Egypt, Sinai, Holy Land and Greece.

Vol. XI. Asiatic Islands: Philippines, Borneo, East Indies, Java, Batavia, Celebes, Amboyna, Australasia, New Holland.

Vol. XII. North America: Columbus, Frobisher's voyages, Raleigh, New France and Canada.

Vol. XIII. North America: Canada, Guaxaca (Oaxaca).

Vol. XIV. South America: Peru, Chile, Brazil and Guiana.

Vol. XV. Africa: Abyssinia, DarFur, Egypt, West Barbary, Mequinez.

Vol. XVI. Africa: Cape of Good Hope, Congo, Angola, Guinea, Senegal, Ethiopia, Madagascar, Canary Islands.

Vol. XVII. Catalogue and Index.

— Modern geography. A description of the empires, kingdoms, states, and colonies; with the oceans, seas and isles; in all parts of the world: including the most recent discoveries, ... The astronomical introduction by the Rev. S. Vince, ... A new edition, greatly enlarged. *London: printed for T. Cadell and W. Davies; and Longman, Hurst, Rees, and Orme, 1807.* 3v. (739, 820, 1006p.); plates; maps.　　IFP354

Pitton de Tournefort, Joseph. A voyage into the Levant: perform'd by command of the late French king. Containing the antient and modern state of the islands of the archipelago; as also of Constantinople, the coasts of the Black Sea, Armenia, Georgia, the frontiers of Persia, and Asia Minor. *London: printed for D. Browne, A. Bell, J. Darby, A. Bettesworth, J. Pemberton, C. Rivington, J. Hooke, R. Cruttenden and T. Cox, J. Battley, E. Symon, 1718.* 2v. (402, 398p.); plates (some folding); maps.

Includes a biography of Tournefort, chief botanist to the French King.

Previous owner: Lee Warly (1779).　　IFP355

Pococke, Richard. A description of the East, and some other countries. *London: printed for the author, by W. Bowyer; and sold by J. and P. Knapton, W. Innys, W. Meadows, G. Hawkins, S. Birt, T. Longman, C. Hitch, R. Dodsley, J. Nourse, and J. Rivington, 1743 [–1745].* 2v. (310; 268, 308p.); plates (some folding); diagrams; maps.

Vol. 1: 'Observations on Egypt'; vol. 2, pt 1: 'Observations on Palæstine, Syria, Mesopotamia, Cyprus, and Candia'; pt 2: 'Observations on the islands of the Archepelago, Asia Minor, Thrace, Greece'.

Three copies. Previous owners: 1) Lee Warly (1777); 2) bookplates of M. Wall, M.D., F.R.S.; Charles Forster, B.D.; Benjamin Harrison.　　IFP356

Poivre, Pierre. Travels of a philosopher: or, observations on the manners and arts of various nations in Africa and Asia. Translated from the French. *London: printed for T. Becket and Co., 1769.* vi, [2], 191, [1]p.
Poivre had been French envoy to the king of Cochin-China, and then intendant of Mauritius. Includes descriptions of West Africa, Madagascar, Malaysia, and China, with particular emphasis on the agriculture of all parts of the world. IFP357

Poole, Sophia. The English woman in Egypt: letters from Cairo, written during a residence there in 1842, 3, & 4. with E.W. Lane, ... by his sister. *London: Charles Knight and Co., 1844.* 2v, (232, 240p.); plates; maps.
The letters published here give particular insight into the situation and expectations of women, western or otherwise, with references to marriage customs, harems, etc. With appendices by E.W. Lane. IFP358

— The English woman in Egypt: letters from Cairo, written during a residence there in 1845–46, with E.W. Lane, ... by his sister. *London: Charles Knight and Co., 1846.* [2], 249p.
With an appendix by E.W. Lane. IFP359

Poynder, John. Idolatry in India: six letters on the continuance of the annual payment of 23,000 rupees by the East India directors, to the temple of Juggernaut. ... Reprinted from the Church and State Gazette. *London: William Edward Painter, 1848.* 23p.
Final verso folded and addressed to 'Sir R.H. Inglis Bart, Bedford Square' with a penny stamp, franked. IFP360

Pratapa Simha, *Rajah of Sattara*. A letter to the Right Hon. Sir Henry Hardinge, ... Governor-General of India, ... from His Highness Purtaub Shean, Rajah of Sattara, now in exile at Benares. *London: printed by Alex. Munro, for Rungo Bapojee (Agent of His Highness the Rajah of Sattara), 1845.* [2], 42p.
Signed by Rungo Bapojee as vakil. From the Rajah whose deposition caused a controversy.
With an autograph letter to Sir R. H. Inglis signed 'Rungo Bapojee'. IFP361

Price, *Captain* **Joseph**. The Saddle put on the right horse; or, an enquiry into the reason why certain persons have been denominated Nabobs; with an arrangement of those gentlemen into their proper classes, of real, spurious, reputed, or mushroom nabobs. Concluding with a few reflections on the present state of our Asiatic affairs. By the author of the Vindication of Gen. Richard Smith. *London: printed for the author; and to be had of John Stockdale; Scratchard and Whitaker; and Mr Sewell, 1783.* [4], 111, [1]p.
Author from Halkett and Laing. IFP362

Prinsep, Henry Thoby. The India question in 1853. *London: Wm. H. Allen & Co., 1853.* [2], 111p.
Concerns the Act for the renewal of the East India Company's Charter. IFP363

Pritchard, John. Narratives of John Pritchard, Pierre Chrysologue Pambrun, and Frederick Damien Heurter, respecting the aggressions of the North-West Company, against the Earl of Selkirk's settlement upon Red River. *[London?]: [1819?].* [4], 91, [1]p.
Includes discussion of the reaction of the colonisers to the native population, the behaviour observed by the settlers, and the treatment they received. IFP364

Proposal for forming a society for promoting the civilization and improvement of the North-American Indians, within the British boundary. *London: printed by J. Brettell, 1806.* 24p.

Includes details of previous attempts to 'civilize' the Indians, and is valuable for the study of colonial contact between them and the British. Half-title: 'Proposal for forming a society for civilizing and improving the North-American Indians, within the British boundary'.   IFP365

Proprietor, A. *See*: **Twining, Thomas***, A letter***; Two letters to the proprietors.**

Purchas, Samuel, *the Elder.* Purchas his pilgrimage. Or relations of the world and the religions observed in all ages and places discovered, ... In foure parts. This first containeth a theologicall and geographicall historie of Asia, Africa, and America, with the ilands adiacent. ... The second edition, much enlarged. *London: printed by William Stansby for Henrie Fetherstone, 1614.* [28], 918, [36]p.; plates; maps. STC 20506.

Purchas was minister for Estwood in Essex. He inherited many of the manuscripts of Richard Hakluyt, but his collections, illustrated with maps and plates, include some material not in Hakluyt. The originals of the many journals which he edited and published were discarded, so the versions printed here are the only extant account of some of the voyages. He had a reputation as a careless editor. A full analysis of the contents is given for the fourth edition (below, IFP367).

Previous owners: 'Hen. Oxinden de Barham', Lee Warly (1744)   IFP366

— — The fourth edition, much enlarged ... three whole treatises annexed, one of Russia and other northeasterne regions by Sʳ Ierome Horsey; the second of the Gulfe of Bengala by Master William Methold; the third of the Saracenicall Empire, translated out of the Arabike by T. Erpenius. *London: printed by William Stansby for Henrie Fetherstone, 1626.* [40], 1047, [33]p.; folding plates; maps. STC 20508.5.

This is frequently treated as a fifth volume of the 1625 *Purchas his pilgrimes* (see the following entry). It was divided into ten books, of which the first seven deal mainly with the ancient world:

The first book: of the first beginnings of the world and religion: and of the regions and religions of Babylonia, Assyria, Syria, Phoenicia and Palestinia. *The second booke:* Of the Hebrew nation and religion. *The third booke:* Of the Arabians, Saracens, Turkes and of the ancient inhabitants of Asia Minor and of their religions. *The fourth booke:* Of the Armenians, Medes, Persians, Parthians, Scythians, Tartarians, Chinois, and of their religions. *The fifth booke:* Of the East Indies, and of the seas and ilands about Asia with their religions. *The sixt booke:* Relations of the regions and religions in Africa, of Aegypt, Barbarie, Numidia, Libya and the land of Negros; *The seventh booke.* Relations of the regions and religions in Africa. Of Aethiopia and the African ilands and their religions. *The eighth booke:* Relations of the discoveries, regions, and religions of the new world. Of New France, Virginia, Florida, New Spaine, with other regions of America, Mexicana and of their religions. *The ninth booke*: Of Cumana, Guiana, Brasill, Chica, Chili, Peru, and other regions of America. [*Tenth book:*] Two accounts describing visits to Russia and India respectively, and mentioning superstitions, tribal divisions and the emperors and priests.   IFP367

— Purchas his pilgrimes. In five bookes. ... contayning the voyages and peregrinations ... circum-nauigations ... *London: printed by William Stansby for Henrie Fetherstone, 1625.* 4v.; folding plates; maps. STC 20509.

The fourth edition, with an additional engraved title-page: 'Hakluytus posthumus or Purchas his Pilgrimes.' —'In five books' is misleading: the work was 'cut ... asunder in the midst' and is divided into two sequences of ten books, covering the Old and New worlds, each sequence being bound in two volumes. Page references and marginal notes are confusing, as they relate to an earlier state, before the books were divided (see the preface).

The Old World. *Volume One: First Part*: Book One: Voyages made in ancient times, languages and religions; Book Two: Universal circumnavigations, including America; Book Three: Voyages of Englishmen along the coasts of Africa, to the Cape of Good Hope, the Red Sea, Abassinia, shores of Arabia, Persia and India; Book Four: English voyages beyond the East Indies to Japan, China, Cauchin-China and the Philipines; Book Five: English voyages in India, Persia and the Arabian Gulfs; sea fights with Portugal and the Dutch. *Volume Two: Second Part*: Book Six: Voyages and land discoveries in Northern Africa, excluding Aethiopia; Book Seven: Voyages and discoveries of the sea-coast and inland Aethiopia; Book Eight: Travels by land in Palestine, Anatolia, Syria, Arabia, Persia and other parts of Asia; Book Nine: Discoveries by land of Assyria, Armenia, Persia, India, Arabia and other parts of inland Asia; Book Ten: Miscellaneous, including Persia, Turkey and the Maldive islands.

The New World. *Volume Three: Third Part*: Book One: Discoveries in the remotest north parts of Asia called Tartaria, and China; Book Two: Voyages and discoveries in China, Tartaria, Russia and other north and east parts of the world; Book Three: Voyages and discoveries of the north, in Asia, Europe, the Polar regions and north-west America: includes Russia, Siberia, Iceland, Friesland, Norway, Greenland; Book Four: English Northern navigations and discoveries including Greenland, the North-West Passage and other Arctic regions; Book Five: Voyages and travels to and in America, including Mexico and Peru. *Volume Four: Fourth Part*: Book Six: English voyages to the East, West and South parts of America; Book Seven: Voyages to and about Southern America; Book Eight: Voyages to and land travels in Florida, Virginia, and other parts of Northern America, including the Azores; Book Nine: English plantations and discoveries in Virginia and the Summer Islands; Book Ten: English plantations and discoveries in New England, New Foundland and New Scotland. IFP368

Ramaseeana. The Thugs or Phansigars. From the evidence of the Ramaseeana. *London: C. Roworth and Sons, 1838*. [4], 32p.

An account of the attempts to suppress the Thugs, based on the Ramaseeana, 'a vocabulary of the peculiar language used by the Thugs'. From the *Foreign Quarterly Review*, XLI.

Dedication on wrapper: 'Robert Harry Inglis from Lord Teignmouth July 31, 1838'. IFP369

Ray, John. A collection of curious travels and voyages, containing, Dr. Leonhart Rauwolf's Journey into the Eastern Countries, viz. Syria, Palestine, or the Holy Land, Armenia, Mesopotamia, Assyria, Caldea, &c. Translated ... by Nicholas Staphorst. And also, travels into Greece, Asia minor, Egypt, Arabia felix, Petraea, Ethiopia, the Red Sea, &c. The second edition. *London: printed for J. Walthoe, D. Midwinter, A. Bettesworth, and C. Hitch, W. Innys, R. Robinson, J. Wilford, A. Ward, J. and P.*

Knapton, T. Longman, O. Payne, W. Shropshire, J. and R. Tonson, T. Woodman, R. Chandler, and J. Wellington, 1738. 2v. (428; 489, 44, 119p.)

The second volume of Ray's *Travels through the Low-Countries.* Rauwolff's account dates from the 16th century and includes details of the different religious groups in Near Eastern countries. Other travellers' accounts collected by Ray include Pierre Belon, Dr Huntingdon and Sir George Wheeler.

Previous owner: Lee Warly (1782).   IFP370

Reasons to shew, that there is a great probability of a navigable passage to the western American Ocean, through Hudson's Streights and Chesterfield Inlet; from the observations made on board the ships sent upon the late discovery; ... offered to the consideration of ... Parliament. *London: printed for J. Robinson, 1749.* 23, [1]p. IFP371

Reflections on the present commotions in Bengal. *London: printed for G. Kearsly, 1764.* 31, [1]p.

An attack on the conduct of the East India Company's administrators following the departure of Lord Clive.   IFP372

Reflections on the state of the late Spanish Americas; and on the expediency of the recognition of their independence by Great Britain. *London: printed for J. Hatchard, 1823.* 52p.

Concerns the Wars of Independence, 1810–1826.   IFP373

Reflexions upon the idolatry of the Jesuits, and other affairs relating to religion in China. Originally written in Italian. *London: printed by H. Hills, 1709.* 24p.

Variously attributed to C.A. Cattaneo, T. Cattaneo, or T. Ceva (BL).   IFP374

Reid, Lestock Robert. Letter to the editor of the "Daily News," in answer to certain remarks contained in three chapters on Baroda affairs ... since re-published in a pamphlet signed "Indus". *London: Smith, Elder, & Co.; Bombay: Smith, Taylor, & Co., 1853.* 70p.

In reply to IFP42.   IFP375

Remarks on the affairs of India by a "Friend of India", *see* **Shore, Frederick John.**

Remarks on the salt monopoly of Bengal and the report from the Board of Customs (Salt and opium) of 1832. *London: printed by T. C. Savill, 1836.* 68p.   IFP376

Report of a public meeting held at the Town Hall, Calcutta, on the 24th November 1838. *London: printed by Stewart and Murray, 1839.* 52p.

Running title: 'The Black Act Meeting'.

Previous owner: 'Robert Harry Inglis, 2 April 1839'.   IFP377

Report of the proceedings at a public dinner given to his excellency Sir James Brooke ... at the London Tavern ... 1852. *London: Baily Brothers, 1852.* [2], 42p.

Reports Brooke's speech in defence of his reputation as Rajah of Sarawak.   IFP378

Review of a letter of Thomas Twining, Esq. to the Chairman of the East India Company. "On the danger of interfering in the religious opinions of the nations of India; and On the views of the British and Foreign Bible Society, as directed to India". *[London?]: [1807?].* 8p.

From the *Christian Observer?* — In reply to IFP484 and IFP485.

Two copies.   IFP379

Review of an article in No. XXIII of the Edinburgh Review, on Indian missions. Extracted from the Christian Observer of June 1808. *London: printed by Ellerton and Byworth, for John Hatchard, 1808.* 12p.   IFP380

Review of "A Vindication of the Hindoos, by a Bengal Officer," ... Extracted from the Christian Observer, Feb. 1808. *[London]: Ellerton and Byworth, printers, [1808].* 27p. Attacks the idea that Christianity and Hindu religion are of equal worth. The *Vindication* is attributed to John Scott Waring (IFP417 and IFP418). IFP381

Review of "Considerations on the practicability, policy, and obligation of communicating to the natives of India the knowledge of Christianity: with observations on the 'Prefatory remarks' to a pamphlet published by Major Scott Waring: by a late resident in Bengal". Extracted from the Christian Observer of April 1808. *London: printed by Ellerton and Byworth, for John Hatchard, 1808.* 15p.
The *Considerations* by John Shore (IFP434). IFP382

Review of the affairs of India, from the year 1798, to the year 1806; comprehending a summary account of the principal transactions during that eventful period. Second edition. *London: printed for T. Cadell and W. Davies, 1807.* 140p. IFP383

Rhyne, Willem ten. An account of the Cape of Good Hope and the Hottentotes, the natives of that country ... with some animadversions upon the same, by Henry Secreta a Zevorzit. Translated from the Latin ... printed at Schaffhausen in Switzerland. *In:* Churchill's *Collection of voyages and travels*, London, 1732, vol. 4, pp. 768–782.
A short topographical description, followed by more detailed descriptions of birds, beasts, fishes, insects and plants. There are further sections on the inhabitants, their clothes, houses, furniture, manners, religion, laws, etc.

Roberts, David. The Holy Land, Syria, Idumea, Arabia, Egypt, & Nubia. After lithographs by Louis Haghe from drawings made on the spot by David Roberts ... with historical descriptions by the Revd. George Croly. *London: lithographed printed and published by Day & Son, 1855-1856.* 6v.; plates.
Six volumes of large colour paintings and plates of the ancient cultures and antiquities, also including scenes of 19th-century life in the Near East.
Previous owners: signature of 'The Revd J.M. Collard, 1911'. Presentation label in memory of Donald Robert Chalmers-Hunt, 1952. IFP384

Robertson, William. An historical disquisition concerning the knowledge which the ancients had of India; and the progress of trade with that country prior to the discovery of the passage to it by the Cape of Good Hope. *Dublin: printed by John Exshaw, for G. Burnet, L. White, P. Wogan, P. Byrne, A. Grueber, W. Porter, J. Moore, J. Jones, B. Dornin, W. Jones, R. White, J. Rice, R. M'Allister, A. Porter, and P. Moore, 1791.* [4], vi, [2], 349, [15]p.
With an appendix on 'the civil policy ... the arts and sciences ... and religious institutions of the Indians', and a map of South East Asia according to Ptolemy. IFP385

— The history of America. *London: printed for W. Strahan; T. Cadell; and J. Balfour, at Edinburgh, 1777.* 2v. (488, 535p.); folding plates; maps.
Mainly on Spanish South and Central America. Catalogue of Spanish books and MSS at end of vol. 2. IFP386

Two copies (one with books 9 and 10 from 1796 edition). Previous owner: book plate of Sir George Nugent; presentation label in memory of Donald Robert Chalmers-Hunt, 1952. IFP387

— — The seventh edition. *London: printed for A. Strahan, and T. Cadell; and E. Balfour, Edinburgh; and sold by T. Cadell Jun. and W. Davies, 1796.* 3v. (343, 475, 422p.)
Books IX and X are the history of Virginia up to 1688 and New England up to 1652.

Previous owner: Joseph Higginson; label of Edward Rainford, bookseller, Red Lion Passage.   IFP388

Robinson, John Beverley. Canada, and the Canada Bill ... with an introductory chapter, containing some general views respecting the British provinces in North America. *London: published by J. Hatchard and Son, 1840.* 223p.
Contains text of bill. Robinson was Chief Justice of Upper Canada.   IFP389

Roe, *Sir* **Thomas.** The Journal of Sir Thomas Roe, Embassador from his majesty King James the First of England. to ... the Mighty Emperor of India. Commonly call'd the Great Mogul. Containing an account of his voyage to that country, and his observations there. [1615]. *In:* Churchill's *Collection of voyages and travels*, London, 1732, vol. 1, pp.687–737.
Roe was attached to the Mogul's court, and so gives a different perspective from other travellers, including descriptions of the customs and manners of the court and aspects of their government. Concludes with a list of 'such things as Sir Thomas Roe would have had sent him to bestow as presents'.

Rogers, Robert, *Colonel.* A concise account of North America: ... to which is subjoined an account of the several nations and tribes of Indians residing in these parts. *London: printed for the author, and sold by J. Millan, 1765.* vii, [1], 264p.   IFP390

Rolamb, Nils, *Baron of Bystad.* A relation of a journey to Constantinople ... giving an account of divers occurrences; how far the King of Sweden's commission was executed there ... also .. . the state of the Turkish monarchy ... a report made to ... Charles Gustavus. Translated from the ... Swedish. *In:* Churchill's *Collection of voyages and travels,* London, 1732, vol. 5, pp.669–716.
Describes a journey made in 1656–57. Gives details of methods of travel, meals, etiquette, etc. in particular at the Turkish court.

Romer, Isabella F. A pilgrimage to the temples and tombs of Egypt, Nubia, and Palestine, in 1845–6. *London: Richard Bentley, 1846.* 2 v.   IFP391

Rondeau, *Mrs. See:* **Ward, Mrs** (*afterwards* **Rondeau,** *afterwards* **Vigor**).

Royal Asiatic Society. The Journal of the Royal Asiatic Society of Great Britain and Ireland. *London: John W. Parker, 1834–1846.* 8v.
Many articles have plates, plans and diagrams.   IFP392

Royal Geographical Society. Catalogue of the library of the Royal Geographical Society. Corrected to May 1851. *London: John Murray, 1852.* iv, 143p.
Catalogues the Society's holdings, ranging from 16th-century accounts, Purchas's and Hakluyt's collections, to 18th-century expedition reports.   IFP393

— Catalogue of the library of the Royal Geographical Society. May, 1865. *London: John Murray, 1865.* [2], 541p.   IFP394

— The Journal of the Royal Geographical Society of London. *London: John Murray, 1831–[1880].* Volumes 1, 2, 8, 9, 11–14, 27–36 (1831–32, 1838–39, 1841–44, 1857–66) only.
The journal includes early ethnographic accounts from North and South America, Australasia, Africa, Asia and Europe, with maps; also summaries of travel theory and knowledge so far attained of particular areas.   IFP395

— Proceedings of the Royal Geographical Society of London. *London: 1862 [–1882].* Vols. VI–XXII; new series I–IV.   IFP396

Royle, John Forbes. On the culture and commerce of cotton in India, Part I. *London: printed for the author, 1850.* iv, 119p.; folding plate.

With a chart of prices and imports of American and Indian cotton, 1806–1849.   IFP397

Rungo Bapojee. Annexation of Sattara. A reply to the dispatch of the Court of Directors of the East India Company, annexing the principality of Sattara, ... by Rungo Bapojee. *London: printed by G. Norman, 1849.* [2], 99p.

With appendices of the East India Company proceedings. The Rajah of Sattara was Pratapa Simha.   IFP398

— A letter with accompaniments from Eswunt Row Raja Sirkey, Bhugwunt Row Wittul and Rungo Bapojee, Vakeels of his highness the deposed Raja of Sattara, to ... the Court of Directors of the East India Company, and ... the President of the Board of Control ... 1841. *London: printed by Schulze and Co. 1841.* 44p.

Letters accusing the British Government of conspiracy with the East India Company over the deposition of the Rajah of Sattara.   IFP399

— Rajah of Sattara. A letter to ... J.C. Herries, M.P. President of the Board of Control, ... With the treaties, notes, and authorities. *London: G. Norman, printer, 1852.* 53p.

Signed 'Rungo Bapojee' (p. 13).

Previous owner: 'Robert H Inglis 13 April, 1853'.   IFP400

— Rajah of Sattara. A letter to the Right Honourable Sir John Cam Hobhouse, ... President of the Board of Commissioners for the Affairs of India. by Rungo Bapojee. *[London]: 1848.* 19p.

Dated 31 October 1848. Against a *Times* article of 17 October 1848.   IFP401

— *See also*: **Great Britain, Parliament.** *Petition presented to both Houses*; **Pratapa Simha**, *A letter to the Right Hon. Sir Henry Hardinge.*

Russell, Henry. The letters of Civis on Indian affairs from 1842 to 1849. *London: John Murray, 1850.* [2], 104p.   IFP402

Rycaut, *Sir* Paul. The present state of the Ottoman Empire. Containing the maxims of the Turkish politie, ... the Mahometan religion, ... their military discipline. *London: printed for John Starkey and Henry Brome, 1668.* [12], 218p.; plates. Wing R2413.

The author lived in Constantinople as secretary to Charles II's ambassador, the Earl of Winchelsea.   IFP403

The Saddle put on the right horse, *see* **Price,** *Captain* **Joseph.**

Sandbach, Henry Robertson. Letter on the present state of British Guiana. Addressed to ... Lord John Russell, ... Secretary of State for the Colonial Department. *London: Longman, Orme and Co.; and Geo. and Jos. Robinson, 1839.* 15p.

A report on the shortage of labour following the emancipation of slaves.   IFP404

Sandys, George. A relation of a iourney begun An: Dom: 1610. ... Containing a description of the Turkish Empire, of Ægypt, of the Holy Land, of the remote parts of Italy, and ilands adioyning. The third edition. *London: printed for Ro. Allot, 1632.* [4], 309p. STC 21729.   IFP405

— Sandys travels, containing an history of the original and present state of the Turkish empire: ... the Mahometan religion and ceremonies: ... Constantinople, ... the Grand Signior's seraglio, and his manner of living: also ... the religion and customs of the Grecians. Of Ægypt; ... Armenia, Grand Cairo, Rhodes, ... the Holy-land; ... Italy ... The seventh edition. *London: printed for John Williams Junior, 1673.* [6], 240p.; plate; map. Wing S680.

Engraved title-page: 'A relation of a journey begun An.Dom. 1610', 'London: printed for Philip Chetwin, 1670'. IFP406

Sauer, Martin. An account of a geographical and astronomical expedition to the northern parts of Russia, for ascertaining the degrees of latitude and longitude of the mouth of the river Kovima; ... and of the islands in the Eastern Ocean, ... by ... Commodore Joseph Billings, in the years 1785 ... to 1794. *London: printed by A. Strahan; for T. Cadell, Jun. and W. Davies, 1802.* xxvi, [2], 332, 58p.; [15] plates (1 folding).
Sauer was secretary to this expedition, undertaken for the Empress Catherine II of Russia. Contains linguistic and anthropological information, with illustrations. IFP407

Schedel, Hartmann. [Nuremberg Chronicle]. Registrum huius operis libri cronicarum cum figuris et ymagionibus ab inicio mundi. *Nuremberge: Ad intuitum autem et preces Sebaldi Schreyer et Sebastiani kamermaister hunc librum Anthonius koberger Nuremberge impressit, 1493.* [20], ccxcix, [6] leaves; ill., map. Hain *14508; BMC ii, 437; Goff S307.
The author is named in the colophon, where the work is entitled *De historijs etatum mundi.* Woodcuts by M. Wolgemut and W. Pleydenwurff.
Two copies (one very imperfect). IFP408

Schomburgk, Robert Hermann. A description of British Guiana, geographical and statistical: exhibiting its resources and capabilities, together with the present and future condition and prospects of the colony. *London: Simpkin, Marshall, and Co., 1840.* [4], 155p.; plate; folding coloured map.
Includes statistical and descriptive information on the inhabitants, European and native, and the languages spoken by various native tribes. IFP409

Scoble, John. Hill Coolies. A brief exposure of the deplorable condition of the hill coolies, in British Guiana and Mauritius, ... *London: Harvey and Darton; Ball, Arnold & Co.; Hatchard & Son; and the British and Foreign Anti-Slavery Society, 1840.* 32p.
Scoble visited Guiana in 1839. IFP410

Scott Waring, John. The history of the impeachment of Mr. Hastings. *London: printed for J. Stockdale, 1790.* [4], xvi, 120p.
Warren Hastings, the Governor General of India, was impeached in the late 1770s on 20 charges including oppression, injustice, extortion, severity, cruelty and high crimes and misdemeanours, some relating to his dealings with the Rajah of Benares and the Begums of Oudh. Scott Waring entered the East India Company in 1766 and was Hastings's agent. IFP411

— Letter to the editor of the Edinburgh Review, ... In reply to the critique on Lord Lauderdale's view of the affairs of the East India Company; published in the 30th number of the Edinburgh Review. *London: printed for J. Ridgway; printed by W. Flint, 1810.* [2], 77, [1]p.
Title-page dedication: 'With the author's [best] compliments'. Stamp of R.H. Inglis.

IFP412

— Observations on the present state of the East India Company, Sir Philip Francis's letter, and on a publication entitled "Considerations on the trade with India." The second edition. *London: printed for J. Ridgway, 1807.* [2], 78p.
Anonymous: MS note on title-page 'by John Scott Waring'. Letter from Sir Philip Francis to Lord Viscount Howick. IFP413

— Observations on the present state of the East India Company; with prefatory remarks ... as to the general disaffection prevailing amongst the natives of every rank, from an opinion that it is the intention of the British Government to compel them to embrace Christianity; ... and a plan ... for restoring that confidence which the natives formerly reposed ... as to the security of their religion, laws, and local custom. The third edition. *London: printed for James Ridgway, 1807.* lxxvi, lxxvi, 78p.
The final 78 pages are apparently sheets from the second edition.　　　　IFP414

— Remarks on Mr. Weyland's Letter to Sir Hugh Inglis, Bart. On the state of religion in India. *London: printed for J. Ridgway; W. Flint, printer, 1813.* 38p.
Weyland's letter is IFP503 and IFP504.　　　　IFP415

— Supplement to the letter addressed to the Editor of the Edinburgh Review, containing remarks on an article entitled "Affairs of India," published in the thirty-first number of that review. *London: printed for J. Ridgway [by] W. Flint, 1810.* [2], 51p.　　IFP416

— Vindication of the Hindoos from the aspersions of the Reverend Claudius Buchanan ... in his memoir, On the expediency of an ecclesiastical establishment for British India, and the ultimate civilization of the natives by their conversion to Christianity. Also, Remarks on an address from missionaries in Bengal to the natives of India, condemning their errors, and inviting them to become Christians. The whole tending to evince the excellence of the moral system of the Hindoos and the danger of interfering with their customs or religion. By a Bengal Officer. *London: printed by Brettell and Co., for R. and J. Rodwell, 1808.* [4], 171p.
Author from Halkett and Laing ('wrongly ascribed to Charles Stewart').　　IFP417

— A Vindication of the Hindoos: Part the second, in reply to the Observations of The Christian Observer; of Mr. Fuller, ... and of his anonymous friend; with some remarks on a sermon ... by the Rev. Dr. Barlow, ... By a Bengal Officer. *London: printed for and sold by Black, Parry, and Kingsbury, and John Rodwell, 1808.* [4], 218p.
Title-page dedication: 'Sir Hugh Inglis From the Author'. MS note of authorship: 'Chas. Stuart'; BL attributes to Scott Waring. Fuller's pamphlet is IFP162.　　IFP418

Selkirk, Thomas Douglas, *5th Earl.* A letter to the Earl of Liverpool from the Earl of Selkirk; ... on the subject of the Red River settlement, in North America. *[London]: [1819].* 224p.
On the involvement of the North-West Company in the Red River Settlement and its destruction. Includes letters and correspondence from John Halkett, Henry Goulburn, W.B. Coltman and others.
Previous owner: 'R.H. Inglis'.　　　　IFP419

— A sketch of the British fur trade in North America; with observations relative to the North-West Company of Montreal. *London: printed for James Ridgway, 1816.* [8], 130p.
Discusses the trade and exchange between the Company and native Indians, and comments on other merchandisers in the area. Also concerns the Hudson's Bay Company.　　　　IFP420

— — Second edition. *London: printed for James Ridgway, 1816.* [8], 130p.　　IFP421

Selwyn, George Augustus. Letters from the Bishop of New Zealand to the Society for the Propagation of the Gospel. *London: [N.J. Burlington], [1844].* 16p.
The travel report of the bishop whilst setting up his mission in New Zealand, with information of his involvement with the natives.
Three copies. Dedication on front wrapper: 'Sir R.H. Inglis'.　　　　IFP422

Semple, Robert. Observations on a journey through Spain and Italy to Naples; and thence to Smyrna and Constantinople. The second edition. *London: printed by and for C. and R. Baldwin, 1808.* 2v. (208, 254p.); plate; folding map. IFP423

— A second journey in Spain, in the spring of 1809; ... and thence to Tetuan and Tangiers. *London: printed by and for C. and R. Baldwin, 1809.* viii, 304p., [8] plates. IFP424

— — The second edition. *London: printed for Robert Baldwin, 1812.* 304p.; [8] plates. IFP425

Sepp von Rechegg, Antonius *and* **Boehme, Anton.** An account of a voyage from Spain to Paraquaria ... containing a description of all the remarkable things, and the inhabitants, as well as of the missioners residing in that country. Translated from the High Dutch. Nuremberg, 1697. *In:* Churchill's *Collection of voyages and travels*, London, 1732, vol. 4, pp. 596–622.
By two German Jesuits. Includes a description of Buenos Aires and the River Plate.

Serampore Mission. Seventh memoir respecting the translations of the sacred Scriptures into the languages of India ... by the Brethren at Serampore. *London: Cox and Baylis, [1822?].* 45, [3]p., map.
Map shows the linguistic geography of the Indian sub-continent. IFP426

Seton, *Sir* Alexander. The memorial of Sir Alexander Seton, Baronet, to ... the honorable Court of Directors, of the United Company of Merchants of England trading to the East Indies. *Calcutta: printed at the Mirror Press, [1810?].* 152, [1]p.
Seton's appeal against dismissal from the Company. IFP427

Shaw, Thomas. Travels or observations relating to several parts of Barbary and the Levant. *Oxford: printed at the Theatre, 1738.* [8], xv, [1], 442, 60, [8]p.; plates (some folding); maps.
Descriptions of the geography, natural history and the people in northern Africa.
Two copies: previous owner: Lee Warly (1759). IFP428

— A supplement to a book entituled Travels, or observations, &c. wherein some objections, lately made against it, are fully considered and answered. *Oxford: at the Theatre, 1746.* [2], XIV, 112p.; plates (some folding).
Includes maps and lithographs, describing Egypt and the Near East.
Previous owner: Lee Warly (1775). IFP429

Sheffield, John Baker Holroyd, *Earl of.* Observations on the commerce of the American States. By John Lord Sheffield. With an appendix; containing tables of the imports and exports of Great Britain from 1700 to 1783. Also, the exports of America, &c. The sixth edition, enlarged. *London: printed for J. Debrett, 1784.* [4], xlvii, [1], 345, [39], 24p.; folding plates. IFP430

Shepherd, Henry. The following memorials and letters are not committed to print from a motive of disrespect to the Court, but as being more readily perused than if in manuscript form ... *[London?]: [1828?].* 16p.
Controversial work addressed to the directors of the East India Company, in letter form, regarding the state of the church in India and Calcutta. IFP431

— The inefficiency of the ecclesiastical establishment of India considered, in reference to the expediency of appointing a second bishop. With further remarks on the practicability of abolishing suttees. Second edition. *London: Hatchard and Son, 1829.* [4], 98, [2]p.
Two copies. IFP432

Shore, Frederick John. Remarks on the affairs of India by a "Friend of India". *London: 1852.* 90p.

On the relationship between Westminster and the East India Company. Author from Halkett and Laing.   IFP433

Shore, John, *Baron Teignmouth.* Considerations on the practicability, policy, and obligation of communicating to the natives of India the knowledge of Christianity. With observations on the "prefatory remarks" to a pamphlet published by Major Scott Waring. By a late resident in Bengal. *London: printed for John Hatchard, 1808.* vii, [1], 101p.

Shore had been Governor-General of India. The pamphlet referred to is Scott Waring's *Observations on the present state of the East India Company* (IFP413 and IFP414)

Two copies.   IFP434

A short narrative and justification of the proceedings of the Committee appointed by the adventurers, to prosecute the discovery of the passage to the western ocean of America; ... The report and petitions referred to in the Narrative. *London: printed for J. Robinson, 1749.* 30p.

Extensively annotated in a contemporary hand.   IFP435

A short state of the countries and trade of North America. Claimed by the Hudson's Bay Company, under pretence of a charter for ever, ... *London: printed for J. Robinson, 1749.* 44p.

With a list of barter equivalences for furs, and a weather log.

Extensively annotated in a contemporary hand.   IFP436

Sierra Leone Company. Copy. Grant of land, and Charter of Justice, from His Majesty to the Sierra Leone Company. *London: printed by W. Phillips, 1800.* 39p.   IFP437

— Substance of the report delivered by the Court of Directors of the Sierra Leone Company, ... 1794. *London: printed by James Phillips, 1794.* 175, [1]p.; folding plate; map.

Discusses the establishment of the colony at Freetown and the development of trade, agriculture and labour in Sierra Leone, as well the continued problems with slavers.

                                                                                    IFP438

— — 1795. *London: printed by James Phillips, 1795.* 23p.   IFP439

— — 1798. *London: printed by James Phillips, 1798.* [4], 61, [11]p.

With an index to the first five Reports.   IFP440

— — 1801. *London: printed by W. Phillips, 1801.* [4], 59p.   IFP441

— — 1804. *London: printed by W. Phillips, 1804.* 60p.   IFP442

Simpson, Thomas. Narrative of the discoveries on the north coast of America; effected by the officers of the Hudson's Bay Company ... 1836–39. *London: Richard Bentley, 1843.* xix, [1], 419, [1]p.; [2] folding maps in pocket.

An account of the surveying expedition with many details of the people and customs of the Sioux and other native Americans in the Red River Colony.   IFP443

Smeathman, Henry. Plan of a settlement to be made near Sierra Leona, on the Grain Coast of Africa. Intended ... for the service ... of Blacks and People of Colour, to be shipped as freemen under the direction of the Committee for Relieving the Black Poor and under the protection of the British Government. *London: sold by T. Stockdale, G. Kearnsey, and J. Sewell, 1786.* [2], 24p.

With a list of members of the Committee, and schedules of provisions and tools to be provided.   IFP444

Smith, John, *Captain*. The true travels, adventures and observations of Captain John Smith into Europe, Asia, Africa and America from Anno Dom. 1593, to 1629. *In*: Churchill's *Collection of voyages and travels*, London, 1732, vol. 2, pp.327–366.
Smith was taken prisoner during the war between the Turks and Transylvanians, and describes his escape from the Tartars. He travelled across Europe to Barbary and thence to Virginia, the Summer Islands and New England, where he describes the English settlements from 1624–1629. The account concludes with a description of the Leeward Islands.

Society for Promoting Christian Knowledge. Duty and policy of propagating Christianity in India. ... extracted from the Reports of the Society for Promoting Christian Knowledge. *London: printed by S. Gosnell, [1803?]*. 15p.
Draws on the reports for 1787–1803.   IFP445

Society for the Propagation of the Gospel. An address read at a general meeting of the Incorporated Society for the Propagation of the Gospel in Foreign Parts ... on Friday, May 19, 1826. *[London]: [S.P.G], 1826*. 22p.
Includes a statement of the cost of maintaining missionaries in various parts of the world; eg. Canada and the Bermudas.
Previous owner: 'Robert Harry Inglis'.   IFP446

— A statement relative to Codrington College; extracted from the Reports of the Society for the Propagation of the Gospel in Foreign Parts. *London: printed by G. Woodfall, 1829*. 30p.
On the creation of a college for slaves on the Codrington Estates, Barbados.   IFP447

Some Pros And Cons of the opium question; with a few suggestions regarding British claims on China. *London: Smith, Elder and Co., 1840*. 43p.
Concerns the Opium War, 1839–42.   IFP448

Some reasons for the unhealthfulness of the island of Bombay. *In*: Churchill's *Collection of voyages and travels*, London, 1732, vol. 6, p.358.
Recommends the Portuguese fashion of living two or three stories high, as they get fewer diseases than the English who tend to live on the ground 'which indeed prepares so many of them so early to take up their rest in it'.

Sonnini de Manoncourt, Charles Nicolas Sigisbert. Travels in Upper and Lower Egypt, undertaken by order of the old government of France; ... Illustrated by engravings, consisting of portraits, views, plans, antiquities, plants, animals, &c. ... Translated from the French.. *London: printed for J. Debrett, 1800*. [2], xl, 730, [14]p.; plates (1 folding); map.   IFP449

South Sea Company. An address to the proprietors of the South-Sea capital, containing, a discovery of the illicit trade, carry'd on in the West-Indies ... by a proprietor of the said company. The second edition. *London: printed for Stephen Austen, 1732*. 16p.
With an engraving of a South-Sea flotilla.   IFP450

— The report of the committee appointed to inspect ... the ... accompts of the South-Sea Company, laid before the General Court ... 16th June 1732. *London: printed by W. Wilkins, 1733*. 35, [1]p.   IFP451

Speed, John. A prospect of the most famous parts of the world. Viz Asia, Affrica, Europe, America. With these kingdomes therein contained, Grecia, Roman Empire, ... Hungarie,

... Persia, Turkish Empire, Kingdom of China, Tartaria, Sommer Ilands. *London: printed by Iohn Dawson for George Humble, 1627.* 2 pts; maps.

Previous owner: Lee Warly (1755). IFP452

Spratt, T.A.B. Travels and researches in Crete. *London: John van Voorst, 1855.* 2v. (387, 435p.); plates.

A mixture of antiquarian notes and contemporary observations.

Presentation label in memory of Donald Robert Chalmers-Hunt, 1952. IFP453

Stadius, Joannes. *See:* **Bry, Theodore de**, *America*, pt 3.

Statement of the claims of the British subjects interested in opium surrendered to Captain Elliot at Canton for the public service. *London: Pelham Richardson, 1840.* [2], 209, [1]p. IFP454

Staunton, *Sir* George Leonard. An authentic account of an embassy from the King of Great Britain to the Emperor of China. *London: printed by W. Bulmer and Co. for G. Nicol, 1797.* 2v. (518, 626p.); plates (some folding); maps.

Includes descriptions of the people, especially in the royal courts, during the embassy of the Earl of Macartney. Describes places visited en route, including Madeira, Teneriffe, 'St. Jago', Rio de Janeiro, St Helena, Java, Sumatra. IFP455

— Corrected report of the speech of Sir George Staunton, on Lord Ashley's motion, on the opium trade, in the House of Commons, April 4, 1843. With introductory remarks and an appendix. *London: Lloyd & Co.; and Simpkin, Marshall. 1843.* 36p. IFP456

— Remarks on the British relations with China, and the proposed plans for improving them. *London: Edmund Lloyd; and Simpkin and Marshall, 1836.* [4], 43p. IFP457

Stephen, James, *Master in Chancery.* The crisis of the sugar colonies; or, an enquiry into the objects and probable effects of the French expedition to the West Indies; ... sketches of a plan for settling the vacant lands of Trinidada. In four letters to the Right Hon. Henry Addington. *London: J. Hatchard, 1802.* vii, [1], 222, [1]p.

Letters to the Chancellor of the Exchequer revealing differences between the interests of the colonists and the indigenous peoples. IFP458

Stewart, Charles(?). Vindication of the Hindoos, *see* **Scott Waring, John.**

Stoddard, Richard Henry. The life and travels of Alexander von Humboldt: with an account of his discoveries, and notices of his scientific fellow-labourers and contemporaries. *London: James Blackwood, [1860].* 316, [4]p.; [8] plates.

Anonymous; author attribution from New York Public Library catalogue. The early nineteenth-century travels retold, with descriptions of the natural history and cultures encountered. Places covered include the Canaries, Cumaná, Orinoco, Cuba, Peru, Mexico and central and eastern Asia.

Previous owner: Julia Elizabeth Marshall (1862) IFP459

Strachan, James Morgan. Juggernauth: its history, ceremonies, and character, as described by a Hindoo ... With an introductory letter to Sir John Cam Hobhouse, ... President of the India Board, by J. M. Strachan. *[London?]: For Private Circulation, [1849].* xx, [2], viii, 68p.

Includes *The History of Pooree* by Brij Kishore Ghose with own titlepage: *Cuttack, printed by W. Brooks, at the Orissa Mission Press, 1848.* IFP460

— Mr. Groves' brief account of the Tinnevelly Mission examined, in a letter to a provincial member of the Church Missionary Society. *London: Hatchard and Son; Nisbet & Co.; and Seeley and Sons, 1835.* [4], 66p.

Concerns the dismissal of Karl Gottlieb Ewald Rhenius. Tinnevelly is modern Tirunelveli near the Gulf of Mannar in Southern India. For Groves's reply, see IFP179.

IFP461

Strickland, William, *Rev.* Notes on the present position of Catholics in India, being the matter of petitions presented to the House of Commons and ... the East India Company. *London: Burns and Lambert, 1853.* 22p.

An appeal for recognition of the needs of Catholic soldiers in the proposed reforms of government in India. Written jointly by Strickland and the Rev. Ignatius Persico, two Catholic priests who had served in India.

Previous owner: 'Robert Harry Inglis Aug. 3, 1853'. IFP462

Strobaeus, Bilibaldus. *See:* **Bry, Johann Theodore de,** *India Orientalis,* pt 3, 4, 5.

Suggestions on the propriety of re-introducing British convict labour into British North America. By a Canadian. *London: J. S. Brickwood, printer, 1824.* [4], 86, [4]p.; tables.

With statistical tables of convictions for the period 1810–1823.

Two copies. IFP463

Sulaiman, *the Merchant.* Ancient accounts of India and China, by two Mohammedan travellers. Who went to those parts in the 9th century; translated from the Arabic by the late learned Eusebius Renaudot. *London: printed for Sam. Harding, 1733.* xxxvii, [1], 99, [1], 260, [12]p.

With notes and a preface explaining the two early travel accounts. The second part is a supplement by Abu Zaid Hasan.

Previous owners: John Innys (1734); W[illia]m. B. Elwyn; book plate of William Harrison. IFP464

Sulivan, Richard Joseph. A letter to the Honorable the Court of Directors of the East-India Company, from Richard Joseph Sulivan, Esq. *[London?]: [1784?].* [4], 110p.

Concerning Sulivan's dismissal by the Company. IFP465

Sullivan, *Rt. Hon.* **John.** A narrative and statement of facts, addressed to the Court of Directors of the East-India Company, October 1788. *London: re-printed by J. Brettell, for J. Hatchard, 1807.* vii, [1], 32, [18]p.

Appeal against the East India Company's claims for compensation because of activities of the ship *Elizabeth* in the War of American Independence. IFP466

Sullivan, John, *Proprietor of East India Stock.* Second letter to ... Sir John Hobhouse ... conveying the opinions of Lord Amherst, Lord W. Bentinck, Lord Auckland, and Lord Metcalfe, on the right of the princes and chiefs of India to adopt successors. *London: G. Norman, printer, 1850.* [2], 46p.

With extracts from the various treaties relevant to the case of the Rajah of Sattara.

IFP467

The Supremacy of truth. Reasons and suggestions for providing each nation with a version of the holy scriptures. ... Also, a plea for an immediate and careful revision of Diodati's Italian Bible. By "Clericus, A.M.," formerly Scholar of Trinity College, Cambridge. *London: Royston and Brown; Seeley and Son; Nisbett and Co.; Hatchard; Partridge and Oakey; Wertheim and Macintosh; Nutt; Jackson, 1851.* 40p.

In a set of pamphlets on the British and Foreign Bible Society's work and policy. IFP468

Sykes, William Henry. Administration of civil justice in British India, for a period of four years, chiefly from 1845 to 1848, ... by Colonel Sykes, F.R.S. *London: London Gazette Office, [1853].* [2], 34p.

From the *Journal of the Statistical Society of London*, June, 1853. Has statistical tables of cases heard and of appeals (with values). IFP469

— Analysis of the report of Surgeon F.P. Strong of the Bengal army to the Bengal government for 1847, of the mortality in the jails of the 24 Pergunnahs, Calcutta. *[London?]: [1849?].* 13p.; tables.

From the *Journal of the Statistical Society of London*, Feb. 1849. IFP470

— Speech of Colonel Sykes at the India House, Friday, 27th April, 1849, on the annexation of the Sattarah principality. *[London?]: [1849?].* [2], 6p.

Title-page dedication: 'Sir Robt H. Inglis Bart MP. from Colonel Sykes.' IFP471

— Speech of Lieut.-Colonel Sykes, at the General Court of Proprietors of East-India Stock, on the 21st June 1853, on the proposed India Bill. *London: printed by Cox (Brothers) and Wyman, 1853.* 28, [2]p.

With five pages of statistical tables.

Title-page dedication: 'Sir Robt H. Inglis Bart.' IFP472

— The statistics of civil justice in Bengal, in which the government is a party. *[London?]: [1849?].* 31p: tables.

From the *Journal of the Statistical Society of London*, Feb. 1849. IFP473

— Statistics of the educational institutions of the East India Company in India. *[London]: [1845?].* 83p.

From the *Journal of the Statistical Society of London,* June 1845.

Dedication on front cover: 'Sir Robert H. Inglis Bart MP. From Colonel Sykes'. IFP474

Synge, Millington Henry. Canada in 1848. Being an examination of the existing resources of British North America. With considerations for their further and more perfect development, as a practical remedy, by means of colonisation, for the prevailing distress in the united Empire, and for the defence of the colony. *London: published by Effingham Wilson, [1848].* 32, vii, [1]p.

Concerns invasion routes. IFP475

Tagore, Baboo Prosonno Comar. *See:* **British India Association of Bengal.**

Tavernier, Jean Baptiste. A collection of several relations & treatises singular and curious, of John Baptista Tavernier ... not printed among his first six voyages. *London: A. Godbid and J. Playford, for Moses Pitt, 1680.* [20], 87, [1], 66, [2]p.; folding plates; map. Wing T250.

Translation of Tavernier's journal of his voyages to China, Japan, and modern Vietnam. Two copies. IFP476

— The six voyages of John Baptista Tavernier, noble man of France now living, through Turky into Persia, and the East-Indies, finished in the year 1670 ... together with a new relation of the present Grand Seignor's Seraglio ... to which is added a Description of all the kingdoms which encompass the Euxine and Caspian Seas. By an English Traveller. *London: printed for R.L. and M.P. and are to be sold by John Starkey, and Moses Pitt, 1678.* 3 pts (264, 214, 119p.); plates. Wing T256.

The volume consists of 5 books on his travels through Turkey, Syria, and Persia, and 2 books on his stay in India and parts of south east Asia, such as Java.

Previous owner: Lee Warly. IFP477

Techo, Nicolaus del. The history of the provinces of Paraguay, Tucuman, Rio de la Plata, Parana, Guaira and Urvaica. and ... the kingdom of Chili. *In*: Churchill's *Collection of voyages and travels*, London, 1732, vol. 4.
Although much of the religious content of this work has been edited out, as being inappropriate for a book of travel, there is still a strong Jesuit influence, and a good description of the spread of Christianity. Translated from Latin.

Thelwall, Algernon Sydney. The iniquities of the opium trade with China; being a development of the main causes which exclude the merchants of Great Britain from the advantages of an unrestricted commercial intercourse with that vast empire. *London: Wm. H. Allen and Co., 1839.* xi, [2], 178p. IFP478

Thompson, Charles, *Traveller*. The travels of the late Charles Thompson, Esq; containing his observations on France, Italy, Turkey in Europe, the Holy Land, Arabia, Egypt, and many other parts of the world: giving ... the manners, religion, polity, antiquities, and natural history. *London: printed for J. Robinson, 1744.* 3v. (448, 432, 404p.); folding plates (some damaged); maps.
Previous owner: Lee Warly (1744). IFP479

Thornton, Thomas. The present state of Turkey; or a description of the political, civil, and religious constitution, government, and laws, of the Ottoman Empire; ... together with ... Moldavia and Wallachia. *London: printed for Joseph Mawman, 1807.* xxxi, [1], 436p.
IFP480

A true and short account of forty two persons who perished by shipwreck near Spitzbergen, in the year 1646. *In*: Churchill's *Collection of voyages and travels*, London, 1732, vol. 2, pp.381–382.
Sole survivor's account.

Tuckey, James Kingston. Narrative of an expedition to explore the river Zaire, usually called the Congo, in South Africa, in 1816, ... to which is added the Journal of Professor Smith; some general observations on the country and its inhabitants; and an appendix. *London: John Murray, 1818.* [6], lxxxii, 498p.; [15] plates.
Appendixes with a vocabulary of Malemba and Embomma, and information on natural history. IFP481

Turner, William. The history of all religions in the world: from the creation down to this present time. ... the object of religious worship, the place, the time, the persons officiating, the manner, and the parts of worship, &c. ... added, a table of heresies: as also a geographical map. *London: printed for John Dunton; and are to be sold by Edm. Richardson, 1695.* [16], 684p. Wing T3347.
Lists the beliefs of the 'ancient heathen', and the 'modern heathen' (in Asia, Africa and the Americas). IFP482

Turton, Thomas E.M. Remarks on the petition to Parliament of the inhabitants of Bengal and Madras against the Act No. XI of 1836. Passed by the Legislative Council of India. *London: printed by Samuel Bentley, 1838.* [2], 28, xx p.
Appendix with the text of the Act and of the Petition. IFP483

Twining, Thomas. A letter to the chairman of the East India Company, on the danger of interfering in the religious opinions of the natives of India; and on the views of the British and Foreign Bible Society, as directed to India. *London: printed by Hazard and Carthew, and published by J. Ridgway, 1807.* 31p.

Anonymous, signed 'A Proprietor'. Against Claudius Buchanan (IFP77). Thomas Twining was the son of Richard Twining, Director of the East India Company, and was acting sub-accountant general.

Title-page dedication: 'From the Author'.   IFP484

— — By Thomas Twining, ... Second edition. *London: printed for J. Ridgway, by Hazard and Carthew, 1807.* [2], 31p.   IFP485

Two journals: the first kept by seven sailers in the Isle of St. Maurice in Greenland ... 1633, 1634 ... the second kept by seven other sailers, who in 1633 and 1634, wintered at Spitsbergen ... Done out of Low-Dutch. *In*: Churchill's *Collection of voyages and travels*, London, 1732, vol. 2, pp.367–380.

These journals include details of weather and astronomical observations as well as physical descriptions of the country and wildlife.

Two letters to the Proprietors of the East India Stock, occasioned by Mr Twining's late Letter to the Chairman; and some anonymous Observations on the present state of India, urging the suppression of the scriptures, and the recal [*sic*] of the missionaries from that country. *London: printed for Williams and Smith, H.D. Symonds, and Black, Parry, and Kingsbury, by Hollingsworth and Townsend, 1807.* 20p.

Signed 'A Proprietor'. An attack on Mr Twining's 'extraordinary' criticism of the missionaries (IFP484 and IFP485) and Scott Waring's *Observations* (IFP413 and IFP414).

Unverified pencil note on title-page: 'By Mr. Hollingsworth'.   IFP486

[The Universal History.] The Maps and charts to the Modern part of the Universal history. *London: printed for T. Osborne, A. Millar, J. Rivington, B. Law and Co. T. Longman, C. Ware, and S. Bladon, 1766.* [4]p.; folding plates; maps.

Atlas of the known world by area.   IFP487

United Brethren, *see* **Moravians**.

Upper Canada Legislative Council. Report from the select committee of the Legislative Council of Upper Canada on the state of the province. *[Toronto]: R. Stanton, printer to the Queen's Most Excellent Majesty, [1838].* 91, [1], 60p.

With an appendix of documents.

Title-page dedication: 'Sir Robt Harry Inglis from J.B. Robinson'. Robinson was the Speaker of the Council.   IFP488

— Report of a Select Committee of the Legislative Council of Upper Canada, upon the provision made by law for the support of a Protestant clergy in that province. *Toronto: printed by R. Stanton, printer to the King's Most Excellent Majesty, 1835.* 86p.

Title-page dedication: 'Sir R.H. Inglis from J.B. Robinson'.   IFP489

Vâlmîki. Râmâyana, id est carmen epicum de Ramae rebus gestis, a poëta antiquissimo Vâlmîke lingua Sanscrita compositum. ... recensuit ... Augustus Guilelmus a Schlegel. *[London]: [Treuttel and Würtz, Trüttel, Jun. & Richter]; [1823?].* 8p.

A subscription proposal for an edition and translation of the epic Brahmin poem, *Ramayana* or *The exploits of Ramas*.   IFP490

Verancsic, *Archbishop*. Iter Bude Hadrianopolim. *In*: **Fortis, Alberto**, *Travels into Dalmatia*, 1778.

Vespucci, Amerigo. *See*: **Bry, Johann Theodore de**, *India Orientalis*, pt 11.

Viger, Denis Benjamin. Analyse d'un entretien sur la conservation des establissemens du Bas-Canada, des loix, des usages, &c. de ses habitans. Par un Canadien dans une lettre à un de ses amis. *Montreal: imprimé chez James Lane, 1826.* vi, [1], 8–46p.   IFP491

Vigne, Godfrey Thomas. Six months in America. *London: Whittaker, Treacher, & Co., 1832.* 2v. (283, 276p.); plates.

Vigne's account focuses on the European settlers in America, in contrasts with earlier journals describing the native Americans.   IFP492

Vigor, Mrs. *See*: **Ward, Mrs** (*afterwards* **Rondeau**, *afterwards* **Vigor**).

Vincent, William. The Periplus of the Erythrean Sea. ... Containing an account of the navigation of the ancients, from the sea of Suez to the coast of Zanguebar. *London: printed by A. Strahan; for T. Cadell jun. and W. Davies, 1800.* Vol. 1 only. Plates (mostly folding); maps.

With observations on modern explorations in these countries. With a portrait of Vasco da Gama.   IFP493

— The voyage of Nearchus from the Indus to the Euphrates, collected from the original journal preserved by Arrian, ... containing an account of the first navigation attempted by Europeans in the Indian Ocean. ... To which are added three dissertations ... By ... Samuel Horsley ... William Wales ... and ... Mr. de la Rochette. *London: printed for T. Cadell jun. and W. Davies (successors to Mr Cadell), 1797.* xv, [1], 530p.; plates (mostly folding); maps.   IFP494

A Vindication of the Cherokee claims addressed to the Town Meeting in Philadelphia ... 1830. *[Philadelphia]: [1830?].* 8p.

Uncut. Title-page dedication: 'for Robt Inglis from the Author'.   IFP495

A Voice for China; an answer to the question, is the war with China just? To my countrymen, the government, and my Church. By one of her ministers. *London: Nisbet & Co.; L. and G. Seeley; Hatchard and Son; and Hamilton and Co. [Printed by] H. & A. Hill, Bristol, 1840.* 52p.

An attack on British policy towards the Opium war and opium smuggling, with an extract from an edict of the emperor of China in the appendix. The article states the moral, social and economic implications of the British actions in China. Previous owner: 'Robert Harry Inglis'.   IFP496

A Voyage to the island of Ceylon: on board a Dutch Indiaman, in ... M.DCC.XLVII. Containing a succinct relation of the productions, trade, and inhabitants ... with some account of St. Helena ... by a Dutch Gentleman. Translated ... *London: printed for J. Bouquet, 1754.* [2], 23, [1]p.

Previous owner: flyleaf signed 'Robert Harry Inglis'.   IFP497

W., M. The Mosqueto Indian and his Golden River; being a ... description of the Mosqueto Kingdom in America. With a true relation of the strange customs, ways of living, divinations, religion, drinking-bouts, wars, marriages, buryings, &c. of those heathenish people; together with an account of the product of their country ... in, or about ... 1699. *In*: Churchill's *Collection of voyages and travels*, London, 1732, vol. 6, pp. 283–298.

Wade, Sir Claude Martine. Notes on the state of our relations with the Punjab, and the best mode of their settlement. *Ryde: G. Butler, [1848].* [2], 14p.

Concerns the second Sikh War.   IFP498

Wales, William. *See*: **Vincent, William**, *The voyage of Nearchus*.

Ward, Mrs (*afterwards* **Rondeau,** *afterwards* **Vigor**). Letters from a lady, who resided some years in Russia, to her friend in England. With historical notes. The second edition. *London: printed for J. Dodsley, 1777.* 2 pts (207, 78p.); folding plate.
With a further 'Eleven additional letters from Russia ... by the late Mrs. Vigor never before published'.   IFP499

Warren, Samuel. The opium question. *London: James Ridgway, 1840.* [4], 130p.
Concerns Sir Charles Elliot.
Title-page dedication: 'With the Authors Compliments'.   IFP500

Watts, William. See: **James, Thomas,** *The strange and dangerous voyage.*

Wavell, Arthur Gooddall(?). Notes and reflections on Mexico, its mines, policy, &c. by a traveller, some years resident in that and the other American states. *London: J. M. Richardson, 1827.* 71, [1]p: table.
A discussion of the British benefit from mining, trade, ownership and improving political economy in Mexico, with information on the relationship between the indigenous people and the colonisers.   IFP501

West, John. The substance of a journal during a residence at the Red River Colony, British North America; and frequent excursions among the north-west American Indians, in the years 1820, 1821, 1822, 1823. *London: printed for L. B. Seeley and Son, 1824.* [2], xi, [1], 210, [1]p.; [3] plates.
West, a chaplain to the Hudson's Bay Company, records descriptions of the people he encountered, including Indians and 'Esquimaux'.
Dedication on half-title: 'With the Author's respectful Comp^s.'   IFP502

Weyland, John, *M.P.* Letter to Sir Hugh Inglis ... on the state of religion in India, with suggestions for its improvement. *Windsor: printed by and for C. Knight & Son; sold by Mr. Hatchard, London; Mr. Bliss, Oxford; Mr. Thorpe, Cambridge, 1813.* [2], 16p.
Two copies, one with the autograph draft of Inglis's reply .   IFP503

— — *Windsor: printed by, and for, C. Knight & Son; sold also by M Hatchard; Mr Mawman; Messrs. Black and Parry; Mr. Richardson; and Mr R.S. Kirby [London]; Mr Bliss, Oxford; Mr Thorpe, Cambridge; Mr Snare, Reading; Mr. Norbury, Brentford; Messrs. Wettons, Egham, Cherstsey, and Maidenhead, 1813.* [2], 26p.
A later(?) edition in a larger type.
Previous owner: 'Robert Harry Inglis May 25th 1813'.   IFP504

Wilberforce, William. Substance of the speeches of William Wilberforce, Esq. on the clause in the East-India Bill for promoting the religious instruction and moral improvement of the natives of the British Dominions in India ... 1813. *London: printed for John Hatchard; J. Butterworth; and Cadell and Davies, 1813.* vii, [1], 109, [2]p.
Dedication on half-title: 'From the Author'.   IFP505

Wilcocke, Samuel Hull. Notice respecting the boundary between His Majesty's possessions in North America and the United States; with a map of America, ... exhibiting the principal trading stations of the North-West Company. *London: printed by B. McMillan, 1817.* 12p.; plate; folding map.
Concerns the Red River Settlement.   IFP506

— *See also:* **Halkett, John,** *Statement respecting the Earl of Selkirk's settlement.*

Wilkinson, Lancelot. A brief notice of the late Mr. Lancelot Wilkinson, of the Bombay Civil Service, with his opinions on the education of natives of India, and on the state of native society. *[London]: Printed for private circulation by Smith, Elder & Co., 1853.* 15p.

Extracts from *The Friend of India* (Calcutta), December 9, 1841.

Previous owner: 'Robert Harry Inglis 1 June 1853'.   IFP507

Williams, John, *Archdeacon of Cardigan.* Two essays on the geography of ancient Asia; intended partly to illustrate the campaigns of Alexander, and the Anabasis of Xenophon. *London: John Murray, 1829.* viii, 325, [3], 24p., [2] plates; folding maps.

Contains some observations on the modern geography. A catalogue of works on 'Voyages and Travels' published by Murray at the back.   IFP508

Williams, Samuel Wells. The Middle Kingdom; a survey of the geography, government, education, social life, arts, religion, &c. of the Chinese Empire and its inhabitants. Second edition. *New York: George Palmer Putnam, and London, 1848.* 2v. (590, 614p.); plates.

A very wide-ranging account of Chinese history, including the language and literature, and European contacts.

Dedication on fly-leaf: 'To the Cathedral Library of Canterbury from Henry Stevens of Vermont, U.S. America, as a small acknowledgment of the Courtesy of Rev. J. Stratton in kindly exhibiting the Library to a stranger. Morley's Hotel. London. June 15. 1849.'

IFP509

Williams, William, *Bp.* Letter to the Right Honorable the Earl of Chichester. *[Not published], 1851.*

Addressed to the Earl of Chichester, President of the Church Missionary Society, dated 'Southwell, Notts, Dec. 20, 1851' and marked 'Not published'. Includes chronological tables of the dispute about land ownership by the New Zealand missionaries.   IFP510

— Three letters addressed to the Right Hon. the Earl of Chichester, president of the Church Missionary Society, relative to the charges brought against the New Zealand Mission. *London: [Church Missionary Society?], 1845.* 44p.

In answer to Joseph Somes (IFP172) and Dandeson Coates (IFP99). Williams discusses issues relating to the spreading of culture and religion, its effects on land rights and social consequences of, for example, the disproportionate number of male missionaries mixing with the native populations.   IFP511

Willyams, Cooper. A voyage up the Mediterranean in ... the Swiftsure, one of the squadron under the command of ... Sir Horatio Nelson, ... with a description of the Battle of the Nile ... 1798. *London: printed by T. Bensley, for J. White, 1802.* xxiii, [1], 309p.; 43 plates; maps.

Willyams was chaplain of the Swiftsure.   IFP512

Wolff, Joseph. Researches and missionary labours among the Jews, Mohammedans, and other sects, ... during his travels between the years 1831 and 1834, from Malta to Egypt, Constantinople, Armenia, Persia, Khorossaun, Toorkestaun, Bokhara, Balkh, Cabool in Affghanistaun, the Himmalayah mountains, Cashmeer, Hindoostaun, the coast of Abyssinia, and Yemen. *London: published by the author, and sold by Mr. J. Nisbet, 1835.* [12], 523p.; plate; folding map.

In the form of letters and journals.

Previous owner: Robert Harry Inglis (April 1835).   IFP513

Wood, *Sir* **Charles.** Speech of the Right Hon. Sir Charles Wood ... on moving for leave to introduce a bill to provide for the government of India. Delivered in the ... Commons ... June 3, 1853. *London: James Ridgway, 1853.* 125p.   IFP514

Wood, John. New Zealand and its claimants: with some suggestions for the preservation of the aborigines, briefly considered in a letter to the Premier. *London: Pelham Richardson, 1845.* 15p.

Following the petition of the New Zealand Company.

Title-page dedication: 'Sir Robert Inglis Bart M.P. from Lieut. Wood'. IFP515

Wood, Samuel Simpson. An apology for the colonial clergy of Great Britain: specially for those of Lower and Upper Canada. *London: printed for J. Hatchard and Son; Deighton and Son, Cambridge; Parker, Oxford; Emerson Charnley, Newcastle-upon-Tyne, 1828.* [4], 50p.

Criticises the 1819 Colonial Clergy Act. Describes the benefits and difficulties in spreading of the Anglo-Canadian church in North America. IFP516

Woodard, David. The narrative of Captain David Woodard and four seamen, who lost their ship while in a boat at sea, and surrendered themselves up to the Malays, in the island of Celebes; ... also an account of the manners and customs of the country. ... with ... an appendix, containing narratives of various escapes from shipwrecks. *London: printed for J. Johnson, by S. Hamilton, 1804.* xl, 252p.; plate.

Compiled by William Vaughan, principally from Woodard's dictation. IFP517

Wylie, McLeod. The urgent claims of India for more Christian missions. By a layman in India. *London: W.H. Dalton; printed at Calcutta, by Sanders, Cones and Co., 1852.* 56p.

Title-page dedication: 'From the Author, McLeod Wylie Esq. Of Calcutta.' IFP518

Drawn by Lieut. Back R.N.

Summer palace of the Emperor, opposite the city of Tien-Sing
   (Sir Henry Ellis, *Journal of the proceedings of the late embassy to China,* 1817. IFP144)

A winter camp on Franklin's Polar expedition
   (Sir John Franklin, *Narrative of a journey to the shores of the Polar Sea,* 1823. IFP155)

The London Panoramas

WHAT did a mid-nineteenth-century family do for entertainment on a day out in London? If they were at all educationally minded, there were already museums and galleries in existence. One possibility was a visit to Mr Barker's celebrated Panorama in Leicester Square. For over fifty years, Barker and his successors (and his rivals) carried on a business which was as popular as the cinema was at its heyday.

A panorama was a huge painted canvas displayed round the walls of a large circular room, lit from above. The public paid one shilling for admission and sixpence for a printed explanation of the painting (with a fold-out plate and a numbered key). The painting was seen from a central viewing platform reached by stairs from an interior corridor. At its height, the Leicester Square Panorama under Barker's successor, Robert Burford, had three such 'circles' each displaying a different panorama, changing several times a year.

Barker's first panorama in 1792 was a view of the cities of London and Westminster painted on 1,479 square feet of canvas. City views were typical subject matter, as were battles and landscapes. The Cathedral Library's Panorama collection consists of four bound volumes of the souvenir guide books, about seventy in all, apparently collected by the Inglis family between 1815 and 1850. The selection presented here does not include the guides to European sights.

David J. Shaw

Bibliography

Bernard Comment, *The Panorama*, London, 1999 (translation from French).

Stephan Oettermann, *The Panorama: History of a mass medium*, New York, 1997 (translated by Deborah Lucas Schneider).

Egyptian Hall, Piccadilly. Catalogue of the exhibition, called modern Mexico; containing a panoramic view of the city ... specimens of the natural history of New Spain ... at the Egyptian Hall, Piccadilly. By W. Bullock. *London: J. Bullock, 1824.* 27, [1]p folding plate. IFP519

London Museum, Fleet Street. Description of a painting of Jerusalem ... from the Mount of Olives. Painted by E. Donovan, ... original drawing by ... J. Donovan; & ... Pierre Jacques ... taken in ... 1811, 1812 ... open to public inspection, in ... the London Museum, Fleet-Street. *London: Philanthropic Society, [c. 1820].* 8p; [2] folding plates. IFP520

Panorama, Leicester Square. A short description of the island of Elba, and town of Porto-Ferrajo; illustrative of the view ... exhibiting in Henry Aston Barker's Panorama, Leicester Square. *[London]: J. Adlard, 1815.* 11p; folding plate. IFP521

— View of the city of St. Petersburg, taken on the tower of the Observatory. *[London?]: 1817.* folding plate. IFP522

— Description of a view of the north coast of Spitzbergen, ... exhibiting in ... Henry Aston Barker's Panorama, Leicester-Square; painted from drawings taken by Lieut. Beechey, who accompanied the Polar expedition in 1818. *London: Jas.-W. and Chas. Adlard, 1819.* 12p; folding plate.
Captain David Buchan's Polar expedition of 1818. IFP523

— — 1820. 12p.; folding plate. IFP524

— Description of a view of the city of Mexico, ... exhibiting in the Panorama, Leicester-Square. Painted by the proprietors, J. and R. Burford, from drawings taken in ... 1823 ... by ... W. Bullock. *London: J. and C. Adlard, 1826.* 12p; folding plate. IFP525

— Description of a view of the city of St. Sebastian, and the bay of Rio Janeiro, ... exhibiting in the Panorama, Leicester-Square. Painted by the proprietor, Robert Burford, from drawings taken in ... 1823. *London: J. and C. Adlard, 1827.* 12p; folding plate. IFP526

— Description of a view of ... Calcutta; ... exhibiting at the Panorama, Leicester Square. Painted by the proprietor, Robert Burford, from drawings ... by ... Robert Smith. *London: J. and C. Adlard, 1830.* 12p; folding plate. IFP527

— Description of a view of ... Quebec, ... exhibiting at the Panorama, Leicester Square. Painted by the proprietor, Robert Burford. *London: J. and C. Adlard, 1830.* 12p; folding plate. IFP528

— Description of a view of ... Bombay ... exhibiting at the Panorama, Leicester Square. Painted by the proprietor ... R. Burford. *London: T. Brettell, 1831.* 12p; folding plate. IFP529

— Panorama, Leicester Square. Now open, a ... view of Bombay. *[London]: T. Brettell, [1831].* 2p.
Handbill advertisement for Panoramas owned by Robert Burford; advertisement for Strand Panorama on verso. – Date from events advertised. IFP530

— Description of a view of the Falls of Niagara ... exhibiting at the Panorama, Leicester Square. Painted by the proprietor, Robert Burford, from drawings taken by him in ... 1832. *London: T. Brettell, 1833.* 12p; folding plate. IFP531

— Description of a view of the Great Temple of Karnak and ... city of Thebes ... exhibiting at the Panorama, Leicester Square. Painted by the proprietor, Robert Burford, from drawings ... by ... F. Catherwood ... 1833. *London: Geo. Nichols, [1833?].* 16p; folding plate. IFP532

— Description of a view of the continent of Boothia, discovered by Captain Ross, in ... the Polar regions ... exhibiting at the Panorama, Leicester Square. Painted by the proprietor, Robert Burford, from drawings ... by Captain Ross ... 1830. *London: J. & G. Nichols, 1834.* 16p; ill; folding plate.   IFP533

— Description of a view of the city of Jerusalem ... exhibiting at the Panorama, Leicester Square. Painted by the proprietor, Robert Burford, from drawings taken in 1834, by ... F. Catherwood. *London: T. Brettell,1835.* 12p; folding plate.   IFP534

— Description of a view of ... Lima, ... exhibiting at the Panorama, Leicester Square. Painted by the proprietor, Robert Burford, from drawings ... by ... W. Smyth ... 1834. *London: T. Brettell, 1836.* 12p; folding plate.   IFP535

— Description of a view of Canton ... River Tigress ... exhibiting at the Panorama, Leicester Square. Painted by the proprietor, Robert Burford. *London: T. Brettell, 1838.* 16p; folding plate.   IFP536

— Description of a view of the Bay of Islands, New Zealand ... exhibiting at the Panorama, Leicester Square. Painted by the proprietor, Robert Burford, from drawings ... by Augustus Earle. *London: Geo. Nichols, [1838].* 12p; folding plate.
Advertises the Canton panorama, running concurrently.   IFP537

— Description of a view of the holy city of Benares, and the ... Ganges ... exhibiting at the Panorama, Leicester Square. Painted by the proprietor, Robert Burford, from drawings taken by Captain Robert Smith. *London: T. Brettell,1840.* 12p; folding plate.   IFP538

— Description of a view of ... Jerusalem ... exhibiting at the Panorama, Leicester Square. Painted by the proprietor, Robert Burford. *London: Geo. Nichols,1841.* 12p; folding plate.   IFP539

— Description of a view of ... Damascus ... exhibiting at the Panorama, Leicester Square. Painted by the proprietor, Robert Burford. *London: T. Brettell, 1841.* 12p; folding plate.
                                                                                      IFP540

— Description of a view of the bombardment of St. Jean d'Acre, ... exhibiting at the Panorama, Leicester Square. Painted by the proprietor, Robert Burford. *London: Geo. Nichols, 1841.* 12p; folding plate.   IFP541

— Description of a view of ... Cabul ... capital of Afghanistan ... exhibiting at the Panorama, Leicester Square. Painted by the proprietor, Robert Burford. *London: Geo. Nichols,1842.* 12p; folding plate.   IFP542

— Description of a view of ... Hong Kong ... exhibiting at the Panorama, Leicester Square. Painted by the proprietor, Robert Burford ... figures by H.C. Selous; from drawings ... by ... F.J. White ... 1843. *London: J. Mitchell, 1844.* 12p; folding plates.   IFP543

— Description of a view of ... Baalbec ... exhibiting at the Panorama, Leicester Square. Painted by the proprietor, Robert Burford, assisted by H.C. Selous, from drawings taken on the spot by F. Catherwood. *London: Geo. Nichols, 1844.* 12p; folding plate.   IFP544

— Description of a view of ... Nanking ... exhibiting at the Panorama, Leicester Square. Painted by the proprietor, Robert Burford, assisted by H.C. Selous. *London: T. Brettell, 1845.* 16p; folding plate.   IFP545

— Description of a view of the Battle of Sobraon ... exhibiting at the Panorama, Leicester Square. Painted by the proprietor, Robert Burford, assisted by H.C. Selous. *London: Geo. Nichols, 1846.* [2], 16p; ill; folding plate.   IFP546

— Description of a view of the Himalaya Mountains ... Kussowlee, Soobathoo, and Simla ... plains of Hindostan ... exhibiting at the Panorama, Leicester Square. Painted by the proprietor, Robert Burford, assisted by H.C. Selous, from drawings ... by ... George J. White. *London: Geo. Nichols, 1847.* 12p; folding plate.   IFP547

— Description of a view of ... Cairo ... exhibiting at the Panorama, Leicester Square. Painted by the proprietor, Robert Burford, assisted by ... H.C. Selous, from drawings by D. Roberts. *London: T. Brettell, 1847.* 14, [2]p; folding plate.   IFP548

— Description of a view of ... Cashmere ... exhibiting at the Panorama, Leicester Square. Painted by the proprietor, Robert Burford, assisted by H.C. Selous, from drawings taken in 1835, by G.T. Vigne. *London: W. J. Golbourn, 1849.* 15p; folding plate.   IFP549

— Description of summer and winter views of the Polar regions ... during the expedition of ... James Clark Ross ... in 1848-9 ... exhibiting at the Panorama, Leicester Square. Painted by the proprietor, Robert Burford, assisted by H.C. Selous, from drawings ... by Lieut Browne. *London: W. J. Golbourn, 1850.* 15p; folding plate.   IFP550

Panorama, Strand. Description of the view of Athens, ... exhibiting in Henry Aston Barker and John Burford's Panorama, Strand: with ... improved explanation. *London: Jas. Adlard and Sons, 1818.* 12p; [2] folding plates.
Plates lithographed after John Burford's drawings.
Three copies. Previous owners: Inglis (1818); Thomas Gaisford.   IFP551

— Description of the island and city of Corfu ... embellished, in the foreground, with ... costume worn by the Greeks, ... exhibiting in H.A. Barker and J. Burford's Panorama, Strand. *London: J. and C. Adlard, 1822.* 12p; folding plate.   IFP552

— Description of a view of the Battle of Navarin, ... exhibiting at the Panorama, Strand. Painted by the proprietor, Robert Burford, from the official plans. *London: J. and C. Adlard, 1828.* 12p; folding plate.   IFP553

— Description of a view of Hobart Town, Van Dieman's Land, ... exhibiting at the Panorama, Strand. Painted by the proprietor ... R. Burford. *London: Nichols and Sons, 1831.* 12p; folding plate.   IFP554

Society of Painters in Water Colours, Gallery. Elephant hunting. A panoramic view the capture and taming of ... elephants on ... Ceylon. By William Daniell. *London: G. Schulze, 1835.* 16p; folding plate.   IFP555

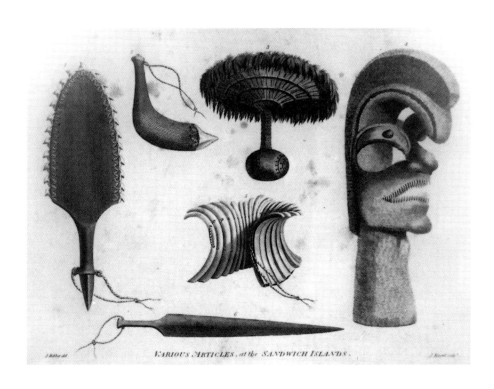

Artifacts from Captain Cook's visit to Hawaii
(James Cook, *A voyage to the Pacific Ocean,* 1784. IFP108)

Sources in Canterbury Cathedral Archives
for the world beyond Western Europe
before 1900

Archives

There are two particularly pertinent groups of documents in the Archives concerning the world outside Western Europe.

Of prime importance is the archive of St Augustine's College, Canterbury (reference U88).[1] Many of the missionaries trained at the college (founded in 1848) were sent overseas. They often sent back letters to their college reporting on their work in locations throughout Australasia, Asia, Africa and the Americas. The college's archive also contains some more substantial groups of papers such as correspondence between the early nineteenth-century Indian missionaries Henry Martyn (1781–1812) and Daniel Corrie (1777–1837), and the books of the Eskimo E.A. Kallihura (c.1832–1856). Kallihura was placed at the college by the Admiralty in 1851. He was baptised in 1853 and left for Oxford in 1855 where he died shortly after.

Secondly, the collection of the parliamentarian Sir Robert Harry Inglis (1786–1855)[2] (reference U210), in addition to the printed books which have been drawn on for this catalogue, contains various journals of his travels to Greece and the Near East in the 1830s and 1840s. There are also a number of charts of coastlines and plans of ports and fortifications of Mauritius, China, Surinam and various European countries from the late eighteenth and early nineteenth centuries which may derive from the East India Company associations of other members of the Inglis family, particularly Sir Hugh Inglis, the first baronet.

---

[1] For the background to the college, see R.J.E. Boggis, *A History of St Augustine's College, Canterbury* (Canterbury, 1907). Further information on the students and their activities abroad can be found in *St Augustine's College, Occasional Papers* (1858–1935).

[2] *Dictionary of National Biography*, vol. xxix (1892), pp.6–7.

Other archival source material for this subject is less extensive. The earliest 'document' in the Archives is actually a cuneiform clay tablet from Mesopotamia of *c.*2000 BC recording a medical prescription, overwriting a previous one (reference U17). The parish archives contain occasional references to collections in parish briefs for those enslaved by the Turks, mainly in the seventeenth century (as in U3/3 (Canterbury Holy Cross), U3/19 (St Lawrence in Thanet) and U3/63 (Wickhambreaux)) and to paupers going to America or Australia (in the 1830s from Preston next Wingham (U3/245)). Other items on this topic include the Eskimos who appear in the late sixteenth-century book of drawings of William Burch (reference Lit Ms A 14), the fifteenth-century letter commending a priest from India (reference DCc/SVSB I/131/1), twelfth-century lists of crusaders going to the Holy Land (references DCc/MS SB A 7 and DCc/Ch Ch Let II/227) and the news of the loss of HMS Babet in the West Indies in 1801 (reference DCc/AL 219).

Artifacts

The cabinets of curiosities collected by John Bargrave (1610–1680)[3] during the mid-seventeenth century comprise mainly an assortment of objects acquired by him on his various tours around Europe as a royalist *émigré* during the Civil War and Commonwealth periods after he was ejected from Peterhouse, Cambridge, in 1643. He returned to his home town after the Restoration and became a canon of the Cathedral in 1662. However, he did venture outside Europe to Algiers in 1662 to rescue 162 English slaves captured from passing ships. Probably on this trip, he acquired some leather boots and slippers, a dried chameleon and a portrait of the Dey of Algiers. One of the grateful rescued merchants also gave him a ceremonial set of a necklet, belt and armlet which he had acquired from the Cree tribe from the south of Hudson's Bay in Canada. Bargrave's collection also contains a string of currency beads from Virginia, given to him by the rector of Chislet (a former American colonist), an Indian tobacco pipe, some Indian Ocean coral and a Persian agate bow-ring.

Also within the Archives are two groups of medieval silks which most likely originated from outside Western Europe, from the Byzantine or Islamic worlds. Archbishop Hubert Walter was buried in a set of silk funeral vestments in 1205

---

[3] Fuller details of the collection can be found in D. Sturdy and M. Henig, *The Gentle Traveller. John Bargrave, Canon of Canterbury, and his Collection* (Abingdon, 1985) and more information about John Bargrave is in S. Bann, *Under the Sign. John Bargrave as Collector, Traveler, and Witness* (Chicago, 1994).

which were revealed when the tomb was opened in 1890.[4] In addition, a great variety of silk fragments were used as seal-bags for a number of the medieval charters of the Cathedral.[5]

Michael Stansfield

---

[4] They are described in W.H. St John Hope, 'On the tomb of an Archbishop recently opened in the Cathedral church of Canterbury', *Vetusta Monumenta*, vii, part I (1893) and N. Stratford, P. Tudor-Craig, and A.M. Muthesius, 'Archbishop Hubert Walter's Tomb and its Furnishings' in *Medieval Art and Architecture at Canterbury before 1220. British Archaeological Association Conference Transactions for 1979* (1982).

[5] G. Robinson and H. Urquhart, 'Seal Bags in the Treasury of the Cathedral Church of Canterbury', *Archaeologia*, vol. lxxxiv for 1934 (1935), pp163–211.

INDEXES

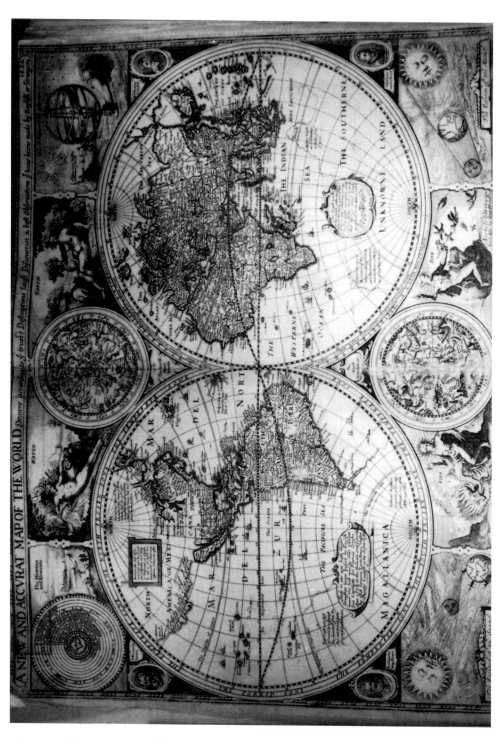

A new and accurate map of the world

(John Speed, *A prospect of the most famous parts of the world*, 1627. IFP452)

Geographical Index

Asia

IFP10, IFP15, IFP68 pts 2–4, 6–10, 12, IFP18, IFP75–76, IFP88, IFP92, IFP95 vol. 2 pp. 327–66, IFP108–IFP109, IFP141, IFP147, IFP197, IFP219, IFP293, IFP331, IFP356, IFP357, IFP392, IFP410, IFP476, IFP477, IFP508

East India Company

IFP29, IFP32, IFP41, IFP47, IFP52, IFP71–73, IFP84, IFP87, IFP111, IFP122, IFP123, IFP125, IFP128, IFP136, IFP137, IFP138, IFP139, IFP157, IFP169, IFP171, IFP196, IFP204–05, IFP216, IFP223, IFP247, IFP256, IFP258–59, IFP261, IFP268, IFP270–72, IFP274, IFP278, IFP307, IFP313, IFP314, IFP315, IFP326, IFP327, IFP333, IFP336, IFP360, IFP362, IFP363, IFP372, IFP376, IFP383, IFP399, IFP411–14, IFP427, IFP465, IFP466, IFP471, IFP472, IFP473

Thomas Twining Controversy

IFP81, IFP149, IFP161, IFP339–40, IFP379, IFP484–85, IFP486

Central Asia

IFP95 vol. 2 pp. 1–326, IFP189, IFP198, IFP296, IFP325, IFP394

India – general

IFP15, IFP18, IFP28, IFP42, IFP55, IFP56, IFP66, IFP68, IFP71, IFP80, IFP86, IFP92, IFP95 vol. 1 pp. 687–737, vol. 2 pp. 1–326, vol. 3 pp.502–822, vol. 6 pp.257–83, p.358, IFP96, IFP102, IFP111, IFP112, IFP120, IFP122, IFP128, IFP132, IFP134, IFP140, IFP152, IFP160, IFP165, IFP168, IFP170, IFP177, IFP191, IFP195, IFP198, IFP201, IFP202, IFP203, IFP207, IFP217, IFP222, IFP225, IFP226, IFP233, IFP246, IFP253, IFP257, IFP258–59, IFP261, IFP269, IFP283, IFP302, IFP306, IFP325, IFP327, IFP328, IFP329, IFP338, IFP341, IFP342, IFP348, IFP349, IFP350, IFP351, IFP354, IFP360, IFP361, IFP363, IFP366–68, IFP369, IFP375, IFP377, IFP380, IFP381, IFP382, IFP385, IFP397, IFP398, IFP399, IFP400, IFP401, IFP402, IFP416, IFP433, IFP460, IFP464, IFP467, IFP469, IFP470, IFP473, IFP477, IFP483, IFP490, IFP494, IFP497, IFP498, IFP507, IFP514, IFP527, IFP529, IFP530, IFP538, IFP542, IFP546, IFP547, IFP549, IFP555

India – church and missionary

IFP23, IFP24, IFP25, IFP26, IFP29, IFP77, IFP79, IFP92, IFP119, IFP149, IFP151, IFP161, IFP168, IFP179, IFP236, IFP253, IFP255, IFP261, IFP299, IFP341, IFP379, IFP415, IFP417, IFP418, IFP426, IFP431, IFP432, IFP434, IFP445, IFP461, IFP462, IFP484, IFP503–04, IFP505, IFP518

Russia

IFP67, IFP189, IFP95 vol. 1 pp. 515–551, IFP190, IFP242, IFP244, IFP245, IFP294, IFP354, IFP367, IFP368, IFP354, IFP407, IFP499

South East Asia

IFP18, IFP19, IFP39, IFP43, IFP44, IFP45, IFP48, IFP60, IFP68 pts 3, 5, 6–10, IFP85, IFP92, IFP95 vol. 1 pp. 453–485, vol. 2 pp. 1–326, vol. 6 pp. 1–40, vol. 4 pp. 573–595, IFP108–IFP109, IFP130, IFP146, IFP152, IFP207, IFP284, IFP294, IFP318, IFP325, IFP354, IFP357, IFP368, IFP378, IFP385, IFP476, IFP517, IFP522

Near East

IFP14, IFP19, IFP38, IFP40, IFP60, IFP61, IFP63, IFP68 pt 7, IFP78, IFP88, IFP92, IFP95 vol. 1 pp. 381–452, vol. 5 pp. 669–716, IFP135, IFP143, IFP147, IFP160, IFP189, IFP198, IFP214, IFP218, IFP219, IFP220, IFP222, IFP230, IFP238, IFP241, IFP242, IFP281, IFP291, IFP300, IFP308–IFP309, IFP324, IFP342, IFP354, IFP355, IFP368, IFP370, IFP384, IFP403, IFP406, IFP407, IFP428, IFP429, IFP477, IFP479, IFP480, IFP494,

IFP513, IFP520, IFP534, IFP539, IFP540, IFP541, IFP544

East Asia

IFP67, IFP68 pt 10, IFP92, IFP95 vol. 4 pp. 573–595, IFP108–IFP109, IFP152, IFP207, IFP234, IFP304, IFP357, IFP459, IFP476, IFP477

China

IFP4, IFP8, IFP57, IFP68 pt 10, IFP89, IFP95 vol. 1 pp. 1–380, vol. 2 pp. 489–500, 721–765, IFP108–IFP109, IFP118, IFP129, IFP130, IFP133, IFP139, IFP144, IFP159, IFP178, IFP243, IFP254, IFP260, IFP264, IFP280, IFP287, IFP288, IFP289, IFP290, IFP294, IFP317, IFP352, IFP354, IFP357, IFP368, IFP374, IFP448, IFP454, IFP455, IFP456, IFP457, IFP464, IFP476, IFP478, IFP496, IFP500, IFP509, IFP536, IFP543, IFP545

Europe

IFP38, IFP63, IFP74, IFP95 vol. 2 pp. 327–66, vol. 4 pp. 762–67, IFP153, IFP189, IFP207, IFP214, IFP291, IFP242, IFP323, IFP370, IFP393, IFP423, IFP424–IFP425, IFP479, IFP521, IFP551

Mediterranean

IFP5, IFP9, IFP38, IFP95 vol. 4 pp. 782–84, IFP180, IFP231, IFP303, IFP406, IFP424–IFP425, IFP453, IFP512, IFP521, IFP552, IFP553

Greenland

IFP95 vol. 1 pp. 487–551, vol. 2 pp. 367–380, vol. 4 pp. 750–762, IFP114, IFP142

Arctic

IFP95 vol. 2 pp. 381–395, vol. 5 pp. 1–664, IFP155, IFP156, IFP237, IFP523–IFP524, IFP533, IFP550

America

South America and West–Indies

IFP11, IFP25, IFP69, IFP83, IFP92, IFP95 vol. 1 pp. 453–485, vol. 3 pp. 1–138, vol. 4 pp. 596–622, vol. 5, vol. 6 pp. 171–239, IFP108, IFP109, IFP115, IFP117, IFP158, IFP175, IFP186, IFP194, IFP199, IFP212, IFP232, IFP249–IFP250, IFP262, IFP275, IFP325,

IFP347, IFP354, IFP366–IFP368, IFP370, IFP386, IFP373, IFP395, IFP404, IFP409, IFP410, IFP458, IFP459, IFP501, IFP525, IFP526, IFP535,

South Sea Company

IFP121, IFP301, IFP450, IFP451

North America and Canada

IFP6, IFP7, IFP16, IFP16a, IFP20, IFP22, IFP46, IFP58, IFP59, IFP70, IFP92, IFP95 vol. 2 pp. 327–366, pp. 501–628, vol. 5 pp. 1–664, vol. 6 pp. 145–170, pp. 241–256, pp. 283–298, IFP103–IFP104, IFP108–IFP109, IFP113, IFP127, IFP130, IFP131, IFP145, IFP164, IFP167, IFP 173, IFP182, IFP183, IFP184, IFP192, IFP199, IFP210, IFP213, IFP215, IFP229, IFP248, IFP263, IFP266, IFP267, IFP276, IFP277, IFP279, IFP286, IFP289, IFP294, IFP297, IFP298, IFP305, IFP306, IFP310, IFP311, IFP312, IFP330, IFP334, IFP335, IFP337, IFP344, IFP353, IFP364, IFP365, IFP371, IFP386–IFP388, IFP389, IFP390, IFP393, IFP395, IFP419, IFP420–IFP421, IFP430, IFP436, IFP443, IFP446, IFP447, IFP463, IFP475, IFP488, IFP489, IFP491, IFP492, IFP495, IFP502, IFP506, IFP516, IFP528, IFP531

North West Passage

IFP95 vol. 2 pp. 381–382, pp. 429–488, vol. 6 pp. 241–256, IFP145, IFP154, IFP224, IFP240, IFP294, IFP345, IFP366, IFP 367, IFP368, IFP371, IFP395, IFP435

Africa

IFP1, IFP2, IFP3, IFP17, IFP33, IFP34, IFP35, IFP36, IFP38, IFP39, IFP68, IFP92, IFP93, IFP95 vol. 1 pp. 553–589, vol.. 2 pp. 327–366, vol. 4 pp. 768–782, vol. 5 pp. 1–668 vol. 6 pp. 1–40, pp. 171–239, pp. 257–282 pp. 355–357, IFP108, IFP110, IFP166, IFP198, IFP221, IFP222, IFP227, IFP228, IFP230, IFP242, IFP273, IFP306, IFP343, IFP346, IFP357, IFP393, IFP395, IFP428, IFP429, IFP437, IFP438–IFP442, IFP444, IFP459, IFP481, IFP493, IFP513

South Africa

IFP95 vol. 1 pp. 762–767, IFP108, IFP239

Egypt

IFP1, IFP9, IFP40, IFP64–IFP65, IFP95 vol. 1 pp. 381–452, 553–589, vol. 2 pp. 625–720, vol. 6, IFP107, IFP198, IFP207, IFP218, IFP219, IFP251, IFP252, IFP265, IFP281, IFP316, IFP324, IFP354, IFP356, IFP358, IFP359, IFP368, IFP370, IFP384, IFP391, IFP405, IFP406, IFP429, IFP449, IFP479, IFP513, IFP519, IFP532, IFP548, IFP553

Australasia

IFP68, IFP39, IFP92, IFP100, IFP108–IFP109, IFP172, IFP193, IFP295, IFP393, IFP395, IFP554

New Zealand

IFP30, IFP31, IFP82, IFP90, IFP91, IFP92, IFP94, IFP95 vol. 4 pp. 622–35, IFP97, IFP98, IFP99, IFP100, IFP101, IFP108, IFP150, IFP151, IFP187, IFP188, IFP200, IFP235, IFP285, IFP320, IFP321, IFP322, IFP422, IFP510, IFP511, IFP515, IFP537,

Collections

IFP68, IFP69, IFP92, IFP95, IFP148, IFP154, IFP181, IFP342, IFP354, IFP366, IFP367, IFP368, IFP395, IFP396

Circum-navigations

IFP12–IFP13, IFP95 vol. 1 pp. ix–xciv, vol. 4 pp. 1–572, IFP126, IFP130, IFP342, IFP393,

Theory of travel and other cultures

IFP27, IFP49–IFP50, IFP62, IFP208, IFP227, IFP228, IFP367, IFP393, IFP446, IFP482

Atlases and maps

IFP53, IFP105, IFP116, IFP176, IFP209, IFP354, IFP452, IFP487

General Index

Index of places of publication

(excluding London)

Provenance index

The books in this catalogue come from three main sources: the general collections of the Dean and Chapter, accumulated during the seventeenth, eighteenth and nineteenth centuries; the Howley-Harrison Library which is the Cathedral's largest single collection; and from the Elham Parish Library.

The general collections of the Dean and Chapter were acquired by purchase and by gift. There is no clear indication here of purchased volumes but some of the names in the list of provenances represent gifts or bequests to the Cathedral Library: Thomas Brockman, Donald Robert Chalmers-Hunt, Stephen Hunt, Henry Lansdell, Henry Stevens of Vermont, and Alexander Wetherell.

The Howley-Harrison collection was left to the Cathedral by Archdeacon Benjamin Harrison on his death in 1887.[6] Within Harrison's library, in addition to the books left to him by his former patron Archbishop Howley, a very important section came from the library of his father-in-law, Sir Robert Harry Inglis M.P. Inglis's books included many bound volumes of pamphlets on what we would now call foreign affairs, many concerning the administration of the East India Company and other colonial territories in North America and Africa, or evangelical and missionary controversies. A great many books recorded as given 'with the author's compliments' come from Inglis's library. Benjamin Harrison's books are so numerous in the present catalogue that they are not indexed separately here.

A third significant source is the Elham Parish Library, represented by the books of its founder, Lee Warly, and his ancestors, John Warly, John Lee, and Henry Oxinden of Barham.

David J. Shaw

Abbreviations: *bdg* binding; *bkpl* bookplate; *ded* dedication; *lbl* label.

Acland, *Sir* T.D. (ded) *1844* IFP221
Allen, John H. *1843* IFP5
Archer, Edward Caulfield (ded) IFP15
Babington, Benjamin (ded) IFP37
Bapojee, Rungo (ded) IFP361
Bayley, E.M. IFP143
Beck, Charlotte IFP158
Beck, Sophia IFP158
Beecham, John (ded) IFP30, IFP31
Blackmore IFP227, IFP228
Boulton, Henry John (ded) IFP46

Brockman, Thomas IFP110; *1844* IFP221; (ded) IFP281
Burnell, A.C. (bkpl) IFP1
Brydges, Harford Jones (ded) IFP7, IFP72
Bunting, *Revd Dr 1841* IFP191
C., I. (stamp) IFP266
Canterbury Cathedral Library IFP109, IFP222, IFP224, IFP225, IFP509
Carrington, Frederick Augustus (ded) IFP82

---

[6] See the Introduction to CANTERBURY SOURCES 1, *The Oxford Movement* (1999), p. xix.